Through My Eyes

You shouldn't be reading this about me! Hell, I shouldn't be writing this about me! You should be reading this about somebody else, and I should be writing this about somebody else. Except I'm not: it is about me.

There are an awful lot of 'me's' there – but I'm rather afraid this is a subject where 'I', 'me' and 'my' are going to dominate, because it's not happening to somebody else.

(Bob Humphrys, on discovering that he had lung cancer)

And that is the problem with terminal illness; it has a seductive power that leads to self-obsession. You arrive at a place where your life is defined by disease. Your only choice is how you respond to the position you find yourself in. This is my diary of obsession: how life was dominated by the cancer that cruelly took over my wife's life and how I struggled, questioned, and lived through it.

Through My Eyes

**A Husband's Diary of Faith,
Hope, Love & Loss**

Stephen Hackney

Authentic

Copyright © 2011 Stephen Hackney

17 16 15 14 13 12 11   7 6 5 4 3 2 1

First published 2011 by Authentic Media Limited
Presley Way, Crownhill, Milton Keynes, MK8 0ES
www.authenticmedia.co.uk

British Library Cataloguing-in-Publication Data

A catalogue record for this book is available from the
British Library

ISBN 978-1-85078-955-0

Cover Design by Paul Airy (www.designleft.co.uk)
Printed in Great Britain by Cox and Wyman, Reading

To Charlotte
Always walk tall darling, knowing
that you were born of one of God's
great children and if life should
ever cause you to doubt,
look to the heavens and remember

Dad
September 2010

Contents

If

IF you can keep your head when all about you
Are losing theirs and blaming it on you,
If you can trust yourself when all men doubt you,
But make allowance for their doubting too;
If you can wait and not be tired by waiting,
Or being lied about, don't deal in lies,
Or being hated, don't give way to hating,
And yet don't look too good, nor talk too wise:
If you can dream – and not make dreams your master;
If you can think – and not make thoughts your aim;
If you can meet with Triumph and Disaster
And treat those two impostors just the same;
If you can bear to hear the truth you've spoken
Twisted by knaves to make a trap for fools,
Or watch the things you gave your life to, broken,
And stoop and build 'em up with worn-out tools:
If you can make one heap of all your winnings
And risk it on one turn of pitch-and-toss,
And lose, and start again at your beginnings
And never breathe a word about your loss;
If you can force your heart and nerve and sinew
To serve your turn long after they are gone,
And so hold on when there is nothing in you
Except the Will which says to them: 'Hold on!'
If you can talk with crowds and keep your virtue,
Or walk with kings – nor lose the common touch,
if neither foes nor loving friends can hurt you,
If all men count with you, but none too much;
If you can fill the unforgiving minute
With sixty seconds' worth of distance run,
Yours is the Earth and everything that's in it,
And – which is more – you'll be a Man, my son!

Rudyard Kipling (1865–1936)

Foreword

by Steve Chalke

A few years ago a friend of mine developed a very aggressive form of cancer. I prayed for her every day for more than a year. Her whole church prayed for her every day for more than a year. While she was ill, I ran the London Marathon and promised her that I would pray the whole 26.2 miles for her healing. I did. But months later she died.

The famous writer C.S. Lewis wrote two, very different, books about suffering and pain. The first, *The Problem of Pain*, written in 1940, is still one of the most logical treatments of the subject in print. But the second, *A Grief Observed*, written twenty-one years later, in 1961, after he had watched his wife suffer and die from bone cancer, sounds a different note.

Shattered by the experience, Lewis penned these words:

> Meanwhile, where is God? . . . When you are happy, so happy that you have no sense of needing Him, if you turn to Him then with praise, you will be welcomed with

open arms. But go to Him when your need is desperate, when all other help is vain and what do you find? A door slammed in your face, and a sound of bolting and double bolting on the inside. After that, silence. You may as well turn away.[1]

The Bible teaches us that prayer is 'powerful and effective' (Jas. 5:16) and calls us to pray for those who are sick. More than that, it's filled with stories of those who were healed as a result of God's miraculous intervention. So, when we cry out in our pain and God seems to ignore us, the questions and confusion are all the deeper.

Why are our hopes, our longings and our prayers so often dashed? Why is healing all too rare? Every day, the cry goes up around the world, 'How can a loving and all-powerful God allow this to happen?' And, in truth, increasing numbers of people excuse themselves from believing in God altogether on the basis that they have 'seen too much suffering' in life. For them a simple hopeful belief in a loving God seems utterly naïve in the face of our cruel world.

There are, of course, those who insist that 'Nothing happens that is outside of God's will.' And, using this as their starting position, they seek to explain the tragedy of each and every untimely and intrusive death through the use of those all-too-familiar 'pastoral' clichés, 'It was her time' and 'The Lord was calling her home.' But even as they are uttered, these statements are found to have a desperately hollow ring. Nor do they reflect the teaching of the Bible or of Jesus himself who taught us to pray that great prayer of longing and, as yet, unfilled future hope: 'Our Father . . . your kingdom come, your will be done on earth as it is in heaven' (Matt. 6:9,10).

Lesley Hackney's death was a tragedy. A much-needed mother snatched from her daughter; a husband robbed of his soulmate; a mother and father suffering the unspeakable pain of their child being taken from them: a wider family and community thrown into mourning through the loss of one of its most loved members. All this is nothing short of heartbreaking. To say it any other way is a denial of reality.

And so this book; this diary of events and conversations, of love and loneliness, of hope and despondency, of joy and despair, of anger and fear, of trust and doubt, kept by Stephen throughout his wife's long illness, is hard to put down. Stephen is an extremely articulate writer but, far beyond that, it is the compelling mix of piercing honesty and raw vulnerability, combined with an underlying faith that is not afraid to ask the hardest questions of God and of himself, that makes *Through My Eyes* an emotional and theological journey that is nothing short of life-changing.

I commend it to you. I warn you that it is not easy to read. But, as I do so, I assure you that in reading it you will be immeasurably enriched.

Steve Chalke MBE
August 2010
The Oasis Centre, London

Introduction

'Stephen, Stephen, come quickly! I've just had a terrible feeling come over me, like something horrible is happening.'

As I ran into the room, Lesley was sat in the swivel chair and turned to face the door, her eyes worried and her face unusually strained. 'What's the matter, darling?' I asked. 'Tell me, what's the problem?'

It was Easter 2003 when she called me into the office where she'd been working, and shared her concerns. They appeared to have come from nowhere and her worries seemed disproportionate to the sensations she had been having on the right side of her face. For some time she'd suffered with slight numbness and the occasional feeling of pins and needles above her cheek. We had spoken with the GP several years earlier and an MRI[2] scan had been taken that revealed no abnormalities, so the situation was left and we got on with life.

Like many other young couples our life had been pretty normal, or at least as normal as it can be for a family whose wife had beaten cancer as a teenager. Lesley and I had first met as she was due to finish six weeks of intensive radiotherapy for a nasopharyngeal tumour[3]

back in 1987. She had come along to a special event held
at the church where I was youth pastor, having heard the
youth group had been praying for her. She was met at
the door by the lady who had invited her, and later that
night we were introduced. I was instantly attracted to
this slim, petite young girl with lovely blonde hair, blue
eyes and gorgeous lips. She was wearing tight-fitting
cotton trousers with a matching blouse and white high
heel shoes, and I remember keeping her chatting for as
long as I could without making it too obvious I was hog-
ging her attention! The only evidence of the treatment
she was undertaking were burn marks to the neck which
she'd tried to cover with her blouse.

Not long after our initial meeting we started dating,
and it soon became obvious that our newly formed relationship was turning serious. It all seemed so simple; we
got on really well and were clearly in love. Any concerns
her family might have had dropped away after a few
months and I began to slip seamlessly into their home –
a transition which now, as I look back, must have been
quite challenging for her parents in light of what she'd
been through. After being together for a year we began
to speak about an engagement, and eventually made
plans to marry in October 1990.

As the results of Lesley's treatment became clear,
signs emerged that the radiotherapy had destroyed the
tumour and, after she was discharged from Weston Park
(the Oncology Hospital in Sheffield), she was routinely
followed up by the ENT[4] consultant in Chesterfield.
Using a camera which he inserted into her nostril he
would check the tumour site and declare it 'perfect'. She
was, to everyone's relief, cancer free.

Apart from these occasional visits to hospital for
check-ups and routine treatments to deal with the after-
effect of radiotherapy, we just got on and enjoyed a life

of happiness. We were married for ten years before our daughter Charlotte was born in 2001, and took the simple pleasures of life centred on home, family and friends as God's goodness.

We moved into our home in Nottingham during November 1997, after a fraught time selling our first house in Chesterfield. Our attraction to the area came many months earlier but our impatience to move to the city in which I was now a pastor caused us to take an option somewhat against our better instincts; a house some miles away. In the end, due to the complexities surrounding the purchase, a few months passed and, one day, whilst driving home from work, I spotted our dream house up for sale on the road we loved. I immediately stopped the car, took down the contact details, pulled up at the closest pay phone and called the agent to arrange a viewing for the following day.

As soon as we stepped through the door I knew this would be our home. It was beautiful – or at least I knew I could make it beautiful. The large, open hallway was impressive with its oak floor and wood-panelled walls. As we stepped into the kitchen and looked down the garden, I was in awe at its length. It was over one hundred and fifty metres long, with beautiful mature trees and a nature reserve just beyond. I was ready to do the deal.

The day we moved was filled with joy. The house needed further decorating and some general TLC, but it was perfect. It felt like God was with us and, as I walked through the door I could hear the local church bells ringing out. We'd been blessed and we both knew it. Not long after, I spotted a card in a book shop with the verse, 'God brought me out into a spacious place because he delighted in me'. We bought it and mounted it in the hallway as a reminder of God's goodness and promise.

And now here we stood, in that house, six years later and about to begin a journey that would change our lives for ever. Lesley was not a woman prone to crying or being overly emotional, so her remarks appeared totally out of character. So out of character, in fact, that I knew they needed to be taken seriously.

That same week we made an appointment to see the consultant at the Charles Clifford Dental Hospital in Sheffield. It started a process that would last over five years and which, to a sometimes greater or lesser extent, I wrote about by way of a diary. Just occasionally at first I would enter in my thoughts about the season we were in and what we experienced. To start with, my diary consisted of more prayers than descriptions of events. During those early years, writing prayers became a means of expressing what I meant, and felt a useful addition to either silent or spoken prayer. As time passed, I noticed that my diary became as much a record of my thoughts and struggles with life and faith, and how to maintain my integrity in the midst of having everything I had been brought up to believe challenged, as it did about prayer. Nowadays, I wonder whether there is much – if any – difference between the two, and see life as an expression of prayer for those who endeavour to walk with Christ.

The entries that follow are as I wrote them at the time, save for a little editing to improve any sloppy grammar. I've not rewritten them so as to allow the progression of my thoughts and prayers to be authentic, including the many flaws. One has to question one's motive in committing to paper one's inner thoughts and feelings. What purpose is served in me spilling my life in print? Furthermore, what purpose is served in allowing people to read the struggles of not only me, but also my wife and daughter?

Part way through Lesley's illness, I coined a phrase which came to define not so much life, but one's response to it. For me, it still holds true. The phrase is, 'Through life some things come to change you; others to be changed by you. Wisdom is in knowing the difference.' For sure, Lesley's cancer had not come to be changed by me, but to change me. And it has, probably more than I will ever know. It has not only changed me physically – I'm now an older and greyer man than I was – but it has changed me emotionally and spiritually. The spiritual process of change is what I was keen to document. As a pastor, I needed to allow my circumstances to shape my life and forge my faith. I needed to know at the end of all this whether I would have a faith at all and, if so, what it might look like. It is the cataloguing of that journey that lies at the heart of this diary.

However, there is an equally valid reason for me to write, and that is to document a woman's courage in the face of fear and anxiety, to allow people to see the effect of illness on the life of an individual and their family; to trace what I have now come to embrace as the reality of authentic faith and its power to sustain and uphold us as we walk through the darkness as well as the light, and for better or for worse, I have written what was true as viewed through my eyes.

Stephen Hackney, August 2010

Chapter One 2003–04

Early Prayers

I said to the man who stood at the gate of the year
'Give me a light that I may tread safely into the
   unknown.'
And he replied,
'Go into the darkness and put your hand into the hand
   of God
That shall be to you better than light and safer than a
   known way!'
So I went forth and finding the Hand of God
Trod gladly into the night
He led me towards the hills
And the breaking of day in the lone east.
So heart be still!
What need our human life to know
If God hath comprehension?
In all the dizzy strife of things
Both high and low,
God hideth his intention.

'The Gate of the Year' by Minnie Louise Haskins.
© *Minnie Louise Haskins, 1908. Reproduced by permission*
of Sheil Land Associates Ltd.

My first record of this journey came by way of a single entry in June 2003 and sat alone in the personal folder of my computer. I include it for the simple reason it establishes the seriousness of the problem we were facing, and shows how this was being established in my mind.

Friday 27 June 2003
Life has been hectic since getting back from holiday and here I am once again seeking to put into place the things that will help me to spend my life on what I believe God desires rather than running here and there simply being busy. I'm sitting here praying and thinking about what is important to me – trying to stay focused in the midst of concerns to do with Lesley's health.

Heavenly Father,
Thank you for the love you bring into my life each day; for your grace and commitment – I am delighted to be your child. Lord, my heart is burdened for my family and I commit them to you for your protection and blessing. Please bring healing into Lesley's life. I wait with anxiety but also peace for the report of her latest MRI scan, and I continue to ask you for good health. I hold to the promise of many years that 'the healing you gave to her is not partial but complete' and rest my heart with this assurance. Please Lord, bring complete wholeness to her face so that all the problems associated with the nerves is eradicated, and I ask that whatever is the root cause of this problem will be lifted from her.
Thank you, Lord.
Amen.

At this time, most of my prayers were still spontaneous and spoken rather than reflective and written. I was coming at life from the perspective of a 37-year-old who was now father to a 2-year-old girl, and life was good. Those first couple of years of Charlotte's life were amongst our happiest times. The impact of what was heading our way was taking time to hit home, and the need for written prayer, which really started my diary, had not yet surfaced. That wouldn't come until mid-2004 onwards, and since I have no further record up until then the following are my recollections as to how this next season of our lives unfolded.

As best I remember, the year progressed with a change of care to a consultant who specialized in max-illofacial.[5] Earlier conversations with a previous member of the team were to establish the possibility of early MS[6] which, over time and with the lack of progressive symptoms, was ruled out. Lesley's problems were specific, and related to one area. The fact that they remained stable was reassuring on the one hand, yet disconcerting on the other. The way of getting a diagnosis was a complex affair, and for the next six to twelve months we had several consultations and various MRI and CAT[7] scans along with numerous discussions. Lesley's old files were pulled out of storage and a full assessment of past treatment was undertaken. Her case was taken to the multidisciplinary team who discussed at length what the problem might be. There were two clear possibilities: either this was scar tissue caused by her extensive radiotherapy when she was 16, or it was a tumour. No one knew, and finding out was not easy.

There were mixed opinions in the team as to the right way to proceed. Everyone recognized that Lesley's case was unique and without protocol. Established forms of practice weren't relevant and the specialists were in uncharted territory. Not knowing the best way to proceed, it was decided in consultation with ourselves that MRI scans offered the best strategy, allowing for close monitoring without the risks associated with the invasive microsurgery required to take a biopsy of the area in question.

As the months progressed and the scans mounted up, our meetings with the team became more worrying. It was during one of our many discussions with our consultant, Jeremy McMahon, that he pulled a replica skull out of his drawer and began to explain exactly where the problem was and why getting a diagnosis was so complicated.

'The area in question is just here,' he explained, 'right at the centre of the head, where all the critical structures which lead to the brain are placed.' He pointed to it with a pencil and said accessibility was extremely difficult and complex. 'The problem, Lesley,' said Jeremy, in a low voice, 'is getting to it.'

Furthermore, the risks for Lesley were compounded not only by the location, but also by her previous radiotherapy. The whole area had been weakened by the treatment and was very sensitive to infection, bleeding and further complications. He then went on to say, 'And if we did the biopsy, we are left with the problem of how we treat it if it is cancer.' The gravity of the situation was beginning to dawn; this was not going to be straightforward. And so, by the time I came to make my next diary entry, the matter was the dominant feature of our lives and prayers.

25 August 2004
Dear Father,
Thank you that I can come to you today to be renewed and refreshed in your love. Thank you too that my approach is based on being your child; I know that I do not need to beg to be heard because I belong to you, despite how I may feel sometimes. Today, I am challenged

to pray and intercede over issues to do with Lesley's health and to ask you to intervene powerfully within her life. Father, I know that you can do this and send your Spirit to work within her. Working from the inside out, I ask that your Spirit would repair the damaged parts of her body. Lord, please cause the toxicity to be lessened within, and I pray that her nerves would not be permanently damaged. I ask for healing in her trigeminal[8] nerve and for restoration of the blood flow into her face. I pray that Lesley will experience divine healing.

Thank you, Lord.

Amen.

Over the years that were to follow, the summer house at the bottom of our garden became a haven for both prayer and reflection. My dad and I had built it during the summer of 2003. We constructed it out of timber sections, and clad it with pine on the outside with an internal plaster finish. I'd designed it for maximum natural light, and so the whole front was a series of joined glass doors. It was fully insulated with a natural pine-clad ceiling and fawn-coloured carpet. Inside there was a reclining chair, small bookcase and glass desk with accompanying chair. The idea was to have a minimalist sanctuary, a place to sit, relax and pray, and it worked really well. During the next few years I would often be found there, working away, reading, praying or thinking. My prayers were still often vocal, but I was starting to make more regular entries in the diary. Like this one in September:

Tuesday 7 September 2004
Today I read these verses from Matthew 6:33: 'But seek first his kingdom and his righteousness, and all these things will be given to you as well.' It's not that you are

against us having things, is it Father, you simply desire
for the priorities of our life to be ordered correctly.
Today, through my prayers, I come to order my life right.
Thank you, Father, for the loving commitment you have
made to us through your Son, Jesus Christ. I enter into
that love today and choose to receive from you the
things you delight to give. Thank you for the Holy
Spirit, and I receive his infilling fresh for today. Help me,
Spirit of God, to be sensitive to you and your presence.
Today, Father, I choose to walk in the fullness of your
Spirit and in the newness of his life. I pray for Lesley and
Charlotte. Bless them both, Lord, and surround them
with your love, and I speak the protection of Jesus over
them. Guard them, Holy Spirit, and keep them in your
presence. Thank you for the improvement in Charlotte's
eczema. I continue to pray that she will be completely
healed from this. I pray for Lesley, and ask that you
would sustain her through your grace. Cause her to
know the healing power of Jesus in her body and help
her to stand strong in you. I pray, through the powerful
name of Jesus, for healing and restoration in her face and
continue to petition you, Father, for her restoration. I
thank you and commit her to you. Father, please confirm
your plans for us; my desire is to build according to the
pattern you would show to us, and I incline my ear to
what you have to say.
Thank you for your love and mercy.
Amen.

Many times I prayed in this way, bringing simple peti-
tions in the hope that God would hear. I knew from the
Bible the importance of continuing to bring our requests
to God, and didn't want to fail in this area. I remember
getting to the place of tiring over my repetitions, and
wondering if God had, too. There are only so many times

you can ask for the same things, and often I felt guilty and wondered if my approach in prayer was simply inadequate. I knew I shouldn't feel like that, that prayer was about the heart not the conversation, but sometimes I did feel that way: inadequate. I can remember it, especially early on, as if the weight and responsibility of prayer was shouldered by me. As Lesley's husband, my prayers could and should have made a difference. The truth is, sometimes I felt like they did and at other times I felt like they didn't. It was not a nice feeling.

Not that all my prayers, or indeed diary entries, were consumed by the single issue of Lesley's health. This next entry comes after tragic news that a young man who had been part of our church for several years and returned home to France, had been killed in a car accident. We were all left stunned, and a small group of us travelled to his hometown to attend the funeral. These are my prayerful reflections on my return.

Tuesday 19 October 2004
Dear Father,
As I sit down to write my prayers to you, my mind is full of the past seven days. It's a week today since we first heard of the death of Sylvain Pardoux.[9] What a tragic waste of a young life – and to what end and purpose? You alone know the heart of man and the destiny of a soul. There is much to reflect upon: the shock, horror, confusion that all make up the emotion of this tragedy. Advice is very scarce at times like this and rightly so, for what can be said? The reasons for his death are unclear, the family, devastated. Having now met them, I pray that you will restore them in their brokenness and help them to find comfort as they mourn. Supporting those left behind is what matters now . . .
Amen

Wednesday 17 November 2004
Last week I was in America, and since getting home I
spent two days with Lesley at the Hallamshire Hospital
in Sheffield. She's been undergoing some tests to see
whether they can find the cause of the problem with her
nerves. It appears that the issue has more to do with
radiation toxicity than anything else, and my prayers
will continue to be focused in that direction.

Heavenly Father,
I commit Lesley to you again today. I pray through the
power of your Holy Spirit to release your word and your
life into her body again. I pray, Father, that she would
know and experience your strength, that these terrible
sensations that she feels would subside, and that your
grace and healing would be released to her in the name
of Jesus.
Amen.

Today's Bible reading included:
    'I will not die but live, and will proclaim what the
LORD has done.' Psalm 118:17.

20 November 2004
Heavenly Father,
Thank you for making me one of your children. Thank
you that you have adopted me into your family. Thank
you that you have raised me up and seated me with
Christ in the heavenly realms. Thank you, Jesus, that
you came and died for me on the cross. Thank you that
you have taken away my sin. Thank you that I now have
true redemption. Please help me, Father, to understand
these truths, to live in the power and the grace of them.
Holy Spirit, please come into my heart again to bring me
into harmony with the truth, to lead me into that truth,

and to guide me. Speak closely into my heart that I
might hear you and know you and understand you.
Give me the ability to walk in your ways, not my own.
Thank you that you are my counsellor, you are my
guide, you are my strength; I look to you again and I
receive you, Holy Spirit, into my heart.
Amen.

24 November 2004
Yesterday I arrived home having spent time with John
Pettifor, one of the elders at the Christian Centre in
Nottingham and a close personal friend, only to discover
the hospital had called to speak to Lesley about the
results of an MRI comparison they'd been examining. It
actually led to several calls throughout the day, the bottom line being that they want to see Lesley a week on
Friday. Apparently there has been some change from the
original MRI, but this wasn't picked up until the neurological team looked at them. We don't know what all this
means as yet, but it led to a dark day for both of us.
Lesley was crying – not something she does too often: it's
not good. Not that I mind her tears, but it suggests that
the pressure is really building up in her mind; the battle
is on more than one front. For my part, I was strong yesterday – anxious and worried, but strong. But today was
my turn for the tears! I dropped Lesley and Charlotte off
at playgroup and then drove around for a while – crying.
I guess I needed to let some of the emotion out. It's just
hard at the moment, hard in every way, living with someone you love and not being sure what's going on or how
things will develop. Who knows where all this will end?
We're looking and praying for better news – but at present it's hard to find. Symptomatically, for Lesley things
are not really improving. The sensations in her face are
fierce, alternating from bad to terrible, but rarely ever

good. It's such a drain on her . . . every day having to face this battle both physically and mentally and never being able to let down her guard. It's tough – life is really tough.

If we are to be honest with our faith, then the whole situation raises questions about divine intervention, and God's interaction in our lives. Today, as I sit to ponder the future, I have no doubt in my heart regarding the nature of a loving God. My questions are more focused on his intervention in our circumstances. God can, but will he act? That is the question. Will we get to see anything beyond what medical science and medicine can offer, or will this simply be the extent of his involvement in Lesley's physical condition? And, if he doesn't – or can't – then how are we to respond to this? Am I to have faith in a God who heals, or simply faith in a God who loves – loves like we do – and more besides, but is equally powerless to act on behalf of his children? Has God truly tied his own hands in the arena of free will to such an extent that he is bound through his own sovereignty so as not to be able to intervene in the affairs of men? The more I consider it, the more I doubt this is fully the truth. There must be another way, a different perspective from which to view the situation.

But, whatever my theology, the reality of what I face today has not changed. The fear, worry and anxiety are all still very much part of the journey. I will not live in denial of what I feel for the sake of professing faith – I will simply choose to allow the faith to rise up in me to help calm those fears.

And so to prayer . . . so Father . . . what to pray?

For Lesley, for her health, both physical and emotional, I ask that her faith would not be robbed through the trial. Help her to stand strong and firm.

For better news from the hospital. Today the consultant is in a meeting to discuss further the scans and how to proceed. Please grant them wisdom in their thinking.

For encouragement for Lesley in her own mind, I raise a shield of protection around her from the onslaught of negative thoughts laced with fear and worry. Help her to stand in your truth, Lord, that she might know your victory.

For healing. Oh, Father, how I pray for some physical sign of healing in her body. I ask for improvement on one front – a sign of divine intervention at work in her life.

For hope – in the present, in the here and now.

And, Father, in your mercy, please remember Charlotte.

Amen.

24 December 2004 – Christmas Eve
It wasn't planned that I'd leave the next entry in my diary for one month, and a lot has happened since. Firstly, we met with the consultant, and he's strongly suggesting that Lesley has a biopsy in January to quantify the problem in her face. That wouldn't be so bad were it not for the fact that the operation to perform the biopsy is complicated and not without risks. Another big decision lies ahead of us. She's booked in for an MRI on 11 January 05 and we'll see how that reads. Meanwhile, Lesley battles on. The problems she faces on a day by day basis are acute, struggling each day with facial and head pain, an eye that won't work correctly and a constant, nagging worry about the future.

Heavenly Father,
I pray for my family and especially Lesley's health. Please restore her, Lord. I'm going to pray for improvement, for

a release of divine power in her life. Father, I want to ask for enough stabilizing in her situation to show no further change in scans, but rather an improvement in what they see. Lord, I stand in the gap on her behalf; give us the victory, Lord. Sustain her health.

Lord, I affirm my belief in you again this day, and choose to trust you above my worries and fears. You have told us to cast our cares onto you for you care for us and Lord, I cast the fears of Lesley and I onto your shoulders and pray for your shalom to fill our hearts again this day.

May your love and peace fill our homes this Christmas-time, and may we walk with you in the power of your Spirit. And Father, I stand strong today in the power of your might against the enemy. I take the victory of Jesus and apply it over our home and lives. I bring Lesley and Charlotte under that divine protection in the name of Jesus.

Amen.

Chapter Two 2005

Living with Cancer – Living with Hope

Wednesday 5 January 2005
This is my first entry for 2005, but on the 30 December I felt God say to me, 'Hold onto your faith, I'm coming through for you.' It was, as is often the case, a time when I was thinking of Lesley's health. I felt quite warm as the words ran through my mind, and obviously on matters such as this I don't want to 'make it up'. I live in the awareness that when you are desperate for God to speak, you can, in your mind, manipulate the situation. However, the 'glow' that accompanied the words suggested to me that the Spirit had engaged my own heart and brought a reality to what had been said. I'm now in a season of waiting – waiting on that word to prove it true. On a positive note, without Lesley being aware of this, the following day she did report a much better time with her head, and the day after and the day after that. Monday, though, was a terrible day. But again, yesterday was better. I'm praying – really, Lord, I am praying to you. I'm waiting for you to come through for us!

And so to other matters: Timing is going to be the key in working through the next ministry phase for the future. The coming months will need to be given over to prayer, conversation and strategy. For my part, I went back to an important passage for me from Joshua for both revelation and solace yesterday, and through it, met with God. I felt him say that during the past ten years I had shown myself faithful, and now, in line with the call in Joshua, I was to show myself courageous. Courage – the need of the hour. It is courage that will lead us to victory. As I glanced on from the passage I noted the following words, highlighted as they were to me both through my own pen markings and the Spirit's promptings, 'Get your supplies ready.' It's a word from God – it's time to prepare to move forward.

Heavenly Father,
I offer my worship to you and thank you again for your love and mercy. I pray for Lesley, for continued improved health and strength – especially in her face and trigeminal nerve. Father, through my prayers I arrest the ingoing progression of this toxicity. I pray that it will be 'so far but no further'. And I ask you to bring about restoration for her. I also commit to you this next scan – my prayer Father is for no change – no change between that last scan and this one, and for some measure of improvement. Lord, I don't want to be naïve with what Lesley is facing, but I do want to rise up in faith and through my prayer to you and stand strongly for her deliverance and healing.

Lead us, Lord, lead us – into our destiny and onto your victory!
Amen.

Wednesday 26 January 2005

Heavenly Father,

I come to you today and thank you that you are truly my Father in heaven. I take comfort and confidence again from the words of Jesus as he taught us to address you in such a way. Thank you that I've been introduced into your wonderful family and I seek your blessing and favour over my life and home today.

I pray, Father, for Lesley and thank you for her. You have gifted me with such a wonderful wife and I continue to ask for your healing grace over her. Strengthen her today and cause your power to be released in her body. And as we await the results of the latest MRI, I continue to stand in faith, waiting on you to deposit your word into our hearts. Deliver her, Lord, from this affliction, and may the outcome of this scan bring us good news. I thank you for the better days over recent weeks and I trust you to 'come through for us'. I believe your speaking about 'coming through for us' put a marker in the ground against which our future progress will be measured.

Lord, I desire neither to be naïve nor unbelieving, but stand with confidence in the face of our affliction – I come through the power of Jesus to address our fears and stand for our victory of healing. I pray specifically that Lesley would regain some weight, that her sensations in the face would ease and the progression of these symptoms would stop. Father, I also pray that what will be shown in Lesley's condition are the result of toxicity and not the symptoms of low grade radiation cancer.

I thank you, Father, for hearing my prayer.

Amen.

Saturday 12 February 2005

Lesley had the biopsy this week, Monday in fact, and things have gone well. The op was successful, enabling them to take the desired amount of tissue for sampling in the lab. We thought we may have received some results on Friday, but the consultant rang to say they weren't back – we need to wait for the coming week, and we have an appointment for next Friday. Meanwhile, further issues have arisen with her health, namely kidney stones and anaemia. This is obviously leaving her further drained and exhausted, and the consultant is seeking to get to the reason for her anaemia in order to treat it correctly. I am very conscious that this is a battle – one that I need to stand in and resist the power of evil and sickness over her life. In fact, I spoke with my friend Rae Galloway only yesterday who also identified the real need for me to cover Lesley through prayer, and to stand over her. There is an enemy at work here, and we must take the battle to him. My prayer today will focus on taking authority over Lesley's situation – this is a time for proactive prayers.

Friday 25 February 2005
Lesley's results were back last Friday. They tell us she has a cancer. This is the first time I've sat down to commit those words to print. I've been avoiding it all week because to commit it to diary seems such a permanent entry; something that remains that we don't want to accept. The meeting with the consultant was hard, and frankly took us by surprise. It's really knocked us back, since we went with a quiet confidence that things were OK – but they're not, not at all. And so now it is confirmed, cancerous cells are seeking to destroy the delicate DNA balance in Lesley's body. What can be done?

The past week has been one of coming to terms with the situation, with lots of tears being shed and many hard and fearful questions asked with few answers. We're playing the waiting game. Waiting on the consultants getting back to us – we've many sessions to attend from here on, the first being an appointment with the gamma knife consultant. There are two possible routes to tackle the particular cancer Lesley has – gamma knife or open surgery. Both come with a cost. Loss of vision or eye completely, loss of sensation to the right side of the face. But there is hope – according to the consultant, we should pursue the options because there is a chance that it can be beaten. Over the range of cancers affecting the skull below the brain, when contained to that area there is a fifty-fifty chance of a cure. So now we know where to position our faith.

The other thing we've learned is the unique situation faced by Lesley. There are only seventeen other recorded cases of this kind of cancer in the world, and none of them in the same position as Lesley. It's a unique case that calls for a unique response and healing.

Emotions are understandably up and down. Well, more down than up, to be honest. And that's for all of us, but particularly for Lesley. She has to cope not only with the information, but also with the debilitating symptoms that abound in her head. What's more, her other health issues are also compounding things. On Tuesday we went to see the consultant for her kidney stone problem. Apparently she shouldn't experience blood loss with a kidney stone, and they want to keep an eye on her. Yes, of course blood loss from the bladder can be sign of a tumour. We are resisting this thought, believing that when she returns there will be no blood in the urine, and that things have settled down.

We've had many difficult and emotional conversations this week over issues concerning Lesley's illness and further progression. At this point it is important that we face the facts of what's going on, but also build hope into the situation. Hope is what we all need. But without spelling it out on paper, we have been completely honest with each other about our worries and fears. This is no time for hidden emotion – only truth, since only the truth can set us free.

Meanwhile, our lives are invaded by family, with both sets of parents taking turns in staying over. We're truly grateful for their help, but we are going to need to maintain a good level of our own family oneness through all of this, otherwise it will become too claustrophobic. Thankfully, Charlotte's happy and involved in play and fun – which is how it should be and how we want it. We seek to maintain her innocence, and we will just have to take each step at a time as we journey on 'Living with Cancer – Living with Hope'.

Once again, I've been to pray for Lesley's healing. I'm simply spending time arresting the situation, and releasing through prayer God's power and authority. This I will continue to do. We're in a war – and I'm putting on God's armour to take the battle to the enemy. 'The reason the Son of God appeared was to destroy the devil's work' (1 John 3:8).

Tuesday 8 March 2005
Heavenly Father,
Accept my prayers as I come to you in humility and faith. I pray that as we go this morning to see the consultant regarding Lesley's kidney and bladder, we will see signs of real improvement. Father, I am praying for real healing in Lesley's body and for a powerful move of your Spirit. Bring restoration to her and I pray that no blood will be in her urine, and the stone close to her bladder has passed. I'm asking you for healing in her body through the power of the name of Jesus.

Thank you, Lord, for being with us, and I ask again for ongoing wisdom for the doctors and faith for ourselves in this challenging journey. I rise up again today, Lord, to confess my faith and confidence in you and to put Lesley's healing under the cross of Jesus.

Teach me, Lord, during this time how to walk fully with you, trusting you with those who are dearest and closest to me.

Watch over us, Lord.

Amen.

Tuesday 22 March 2005

Heavenly Father,

Thank you that the situation with Lesley's kidney stones appears to have significantly improved.

Thank you, Father, for this answer to our prayers that has given Lesley such relief.

I now pray for her face and head. I pray she will receive divine healing from this tumour and that when she goes for treatment the effectiveness of the therapy would be complete – giving her full and total deliverance.

I thank you, Father, for your desire to see Lesley well, and today I join my prayer with your heart to see deliverance. Truly, Lord, I am looking for you to come through for us in this matter – I ask for your victory over her life.

Thank you for the openings that you have given for Lesley to receive such treatment in the top centre in the country.

Thank you, Lord, that this has been given to us easily and that these doors have opened.

Thank you, Lord, for the ability of the medical staff to perform this procedure, and I ask you to look upon her with favour, that the treatment would work powerfully and that Lesley would become a living testimony to your love and grace and healing.

Father, I pray that Lesley would also have improvement in her eye – that the imbalance and double vision she is suffering would ease and that she would have a good day.

In your mercy, hear my prayer.

Amen.

Thursday 7 April 2005

Today I read that 'the kingdom of God is not a matter of talk but of power'.[10] And oh, how we desire for that power to be released in our lives – 'Lord, I need your power.'

Heavenly Father,

I pray for your power to be released in Lesley's life. Release your mercy and healing to bring strength and deliverance. Through my prayers I stand against disease, sickness and cancer, and rise up in the power of the name of Jesus to see her set free.

Amen.

I spoke to the church leadership team on Tuesday night about Lesley's situation. As I'd expected, they were very supportive. Ricky Paul, one of the team, spoke afterwards about trust and thanksgiving – of thanking God for the healing in Lesley's body. I am going to be more proactive in thanksgiving for her healing, without neglecting to really stand for her and over her in prayer. I know that as Lesley's husband this is my role and responsibility and I'm not to take it lightly – and I don't!

Lesley's treatment is set for the 17 April 2005. I'm going to rally everyone to prayer on that day, to focus and fast for a miracle of healing and deliverance. God is able! And our faith and confidence in his ability and desire to act will rise in us.

Heavenly Father,
I thank you for the Scripture that our friend Ruth
Galloway passed over to Lesley during their conversa-
tion last week.

'Blessed are those . . . who have set their hearts on pil-
grimage. As they pass through the Valley of Baca, they
make it a place of spring. . .'[11]

I believe, Lord, that this Valley of Baca will be turned
into a place of springs for Lesley. I am asking, Lord, for
a true supernatural breakthrough in her experience that
will astound all who hear of it.

Amen.

Tuesday 12 April 2005   Sixty days after diagnosis
Today at 5 p.m. we will go to see the elders at the
Christian Centre to receive prayer for Lesley. This is
important for us, and a central part of the faith stand in
respect of healing. It's a positive step in our eyes, and
even as I write I sense an air of expectation. It's an
important step of faith that is not about 'going through
the motions' but a vital part of the healing process . . .

. . . When we arrive at the Christian Centre we are warmly
greeted and taken upstairs to meet David Shearman, the
senior pastor, and the rest of the elders. We enter the room
as friends and are greeted as such, and places are given up
for Lesley and me to sit down on one of the comfortable
brown leather settees. I've sat there many times before, but
for Lesley it's a less familiar environment and everyone is
keen to make sure she is feeling comfortable. No sooner are
we seated than drinks are being offered, which I accept but
Lesley declines.

Central to the two settees stands a large coffee table
with a beautiful arrangement of flowers including lilies,
roses and delphiniums. They are carefully positioned

amongst lots of large green foliage and command everyone's eye as they walk into the room. Rarely have I seen
such a wonderful display bringing calm into a room;
their colours adding to the warmth of our welcome.

'A small gift of love from us all,' says David, as he
leads the others. 'We know it can't take away your problems, but hope they might bring some joy when you
look at them in your home.'

We're both touched by their thoughtfulness. It's a step
they needn't have taken and yet, in the act of giving,
their loving commitment to us as a couple is shown. As
we settle, we share some gentle banter and casual conversation, listening and interacting with each other, but
soon turn to the reason for our visit, and different people ask Lesley how she's feeling. She answers them with
her usual calmness and composure.

'This is not about me,' she tells them. 'It's about
Stephen and Charlotte. I want to be well, to be healthy
for them.'

Without knowing her, you could be forgiven for
thinking the comments are feigned, with a sense of false
humility, but they're not. She means exactly what she
says and her selflessness soon wins the affection of
everyone in the room, leaving us all reflecting over our
own motives – but none more than me.

As we chat and Lesley speaks about her problems and
what she faces on a day by day basis, she goes on to
explain what the consultant has said and how serious
her condition is. It's clear to everyone that the prayers to
be offered need not only to sustain but also deliver, and
so when it comes to prayer a little later the directive is
clear.

We'd gone to see the elders out of obedience to the
teaching of the Bible found in James's epistle. 'Is any one

of you in trouble? He should pray. Is anyone happy? Let him sing songs of praise. Is any one of you sick? He should call the elders of the church to pray over him and anoint him with oil in the name of the Lord. And the prayer offered in faith will make the sick person well; the Lord will raise him up. If he has sinned, he will be forgiven. Therefore confess your sins to each other and pray for each other so that you may be healed. The prayer of a righteous man is powerful and effective' (Jas. 5:13–16). And so when it came time to be anointed, John Pettifor asked if there were any sins we needed to confess and we both took a moment to examine our hearts and attitudes before proceeding. And then, as the oil placed on Lesley's forehead gently ran down her face, they prayed and lifted her to God. It was a special moment, one of humility and grace. Here we were, not in strength but in weakness, trusting that the prayers of others would sustain us.

Earlier I'd prayed my own prayers, trusting that together with their own, something wonderful might happen . . .

Heavenly Father,
I approach you through my prayers, to ask for intervention at the hands of our praying friends. I turn from my sin and any blockage that might arise within me to clear the path for you to work in our lives. And through my prayers ask that you would step powerfully into Lesley's life to bring about the intervention we desire for her healing. Thank you that you are my Father and the invitation, through Scripture, is to approach you on these terms. And I bring Lesley before you today and ask that as she is anointed with oil a supernatural act will take place.
Amen.

Later that day, I thought I heard the whisper of the Spirit in the midst of our trials, saying, 'We are being shaken but we have not been shattered.' I hope I heard correctly and that any shaking would ultimately strengthen us.

Wednesday 11 May 2005   Eighty-eight days after
   diagnosis

It's a month since I last made an entry in my diary, not that I haven't been praying, since at the present time prayer in one form or another is really important to me.

Lesley went for her gamma knife surgery on 18 April, and we are now waiting for improvement, health and good news. Not that it's easy, and over the last few weeks we've been through some really hard struggles. Emotions running high, fear never too far from the door, and worry a constant issue for the mind. It's as if one's default is being tampered with in order to make worry the predominant emotion of life. I perceive that if this becomes the case, then fear is never far behind, with its desire to crush and paralyze the soul – it's something to recognize.

Getting through the surgery experience for Lesley has been traumatic and draining, and yet despite all of that she took it with enormous courage and tenacity, standing strong when many would have been weak and crumbled.

The day started at 7.15 a.m. with a visit from the consultant, and from there it was down to the scanning department and off to have the head frame fitted. I sat outside while Lesley was taken into a small room for the procedure. I occupied myself playing Bubble Breaker on my PDA. She returned about half an hour later having had four sharp needles injected into the skull in order to numb the area prior to screwing the frame into place. It is a vitally important part of the procedure; the head must be held completely still during 'surgery'. From there, we went to a different area for further scans (each one lasting about an hour) and finally transferred over to Weston Park on the internal ambulance for the treatment.

The treatment was a complex affair, with over twenty different positions and 179 minutes of actual radiotherapy delivered to the tumour. The procedure is known under two names, either gamma knife surgery, or stereotactic radio surgery. I think the idea of the gamma knife can be a little misleading simply because no blades are used and no skin is cut. Basically this is cutting edge radiotherapy where the dose is delivered with pinpoint accuracy. It's a procedure that can only be used on the head for tumours less than 3 cm. in diameter.

On arriving at the centre I was amazed by the dedication and professionalism of the people whose care Lesley was under. These professionals are at the top of their game, competent, polite and in control – you need that, of course, when you step inside a room that looks like a set out of *Star Trek*. A series of computers and screens in one room and a large cylindrical machine in the other separated by what appeared like armoured-plated glass, I stood as Lesley was led and positioned in what looked like an overweight doughnut. We kissed, I prayed, and off she went. I left Lesley after she had been fixed to the machine listening to David Hind and Tim Hughes on CD.[12]

I then went off for several hours into the city to wander, make phone calls and pray. Many good people were praying for us on that day. I arrived back on the ward at 5 p.m. and Lesley was sitting up on a bed, her head now free of the frame, and drinking a cup of tea. Normal procedure after gamma knife surgery is an overnight stay for rest and observation, but at 7 p.m. we drove back the fifty miles to Nottingham, exhausted, drained, but home, having negotiated her release from the ward.

Three weeks have passed since that major day in our lives, and we are still up and down. There's been some progress with a lessening in pain, and her eye is now covered which helps with the double vision problem, giving her better mobility. We've made several visits to the hospital since then to get help for her eye, and to get checked over. We hope for continued improvement as the weeks go by.

Yesterday was hard. Lesley's emotions are really taking a battering – and what can you expect? I'm trying to comfort her, but at the same time not being silly with offering things I can't deliver. To do such builds a false environment. I had been standing more confidently recently over the success of her treatment, and maybe overlooked the fact that she is still suffering with terrible fears that haunt and catch her unawares. We then went out together, trying to comfort and support her – I hope it helped. There's so much powerlessness attached to disease.

Today I came to pray and read – to follow through on my devotions – and was up to chapter 11 of John. Verse 4 stood out to me as I read, 'This sickness will not end in death. No, it is for God's glory so that God's Son may be glorified through it.'

We must live from the perspective of the treatment having worked – this is what I felt as I considered the verse. I don't want to be naïve with all of this, but we have been looking for God's word to stand on, and I'm going to take these promptings in that way. I did not manipulate the readings in order to get the verse, and this is my usual practice in seeking to hear from God. I know it's a biggie, but I'm receiving it as God's word for us.

Tuesday 17 May 2005

Yesterday I spoke with an old friend, Hilda Gordon; she said Lesley is being upheld regularly in the Healing Rooms she runs in Norwich. Thank God for people who are standing with us and praying; it makes a difference to know.

Lesley has had some better days over the past week. She's been sleeping better and has lived without painkillers for over seven days. I really thank God for this and pray for ongoing improvement in this way. Something measurable that shows progress.

Heavenly Father,

I lift Lesley to you again this morning, asking for health and strength for her throughout this day.

Thank you for your grace and mercy over our lives, and we put our trust in you. I stand in faith for total healing in Lesley's body from disease and cancer, and for the powerful effect of the treatment to rid her of this illness. Thank you for Charlotte, and bless her in a wonderful way. Give her strength and confidence and help her to mix with other children and grow in self-confidence. I lift her to you, praying for your grace and mercy to watch over her.

Amen.

Wednesday 18 May 2005

Today I read from John 21:22 where Jesus speaks to Peter in reference to John, saying, 'If I want him to remain alive until I return, what is that to you? You must follow me.' It is the personal application of Jesus' words that stick in my mind. The important thing was Peter's response to what Jesus had said to him, not what might happen to John that really mattered. It's true today. It doesn't matter what Jesus is doing in someone else's life,

or indeed church – what is really important is that I am
following him!

Heavenly Father,
I affirm again my own commitment to follow your Son,
Jesus Christ. I affirm my intention to be a true follower –
dedicated and devoted to your truth. So, Lord, strength-
en me this day in the decision I have made, and fill me
with your Spirit that I might carry on with courage and
pure devotion.
Amen.

Saturday 4 June 2005
We spent the Bank Holiday in Torquay, which came as
a welcome break for all of us. Lesley had booked us
and her parents into The Imperial, a five-star luxury
hotel that stood high on a cliff overlooking Torbay. The
view was fantastic, and the hotel in a league of its own.
We all felt really posh and not at all awkward sitting
down for dinner in their elegant dining room with full
silver service, and having our bags transported to the
room.

We met up with David and Lucie Gerry, our friends
who had recently moved back to Torquay from
Nottingham, and went to view their new home. Other
friends were down for the weekend too, so Lesley and I
had chance to go out with them while her parents, Dave
and Val, took care of Charlotte. It was a great few days
together, with laughter and relaxation – and all by the
sea: a bonus!

Last Wednesday evening was hard. Lesley was really
upset and crying with fear and worry. I tried to comfort
her, to help her through that time, and we spent a long
time holding each other and listening to each other's
worries and concerns.

Heavenly Father,
I commit those fears to you today, and draw upon your peace and love to drive them away. I ask that she might have your power and grace fill her life with genuine hope. I pray too for the ongoing work of healing, resisting this disease and standing in the power of the name of Jesus.
Amen.

Tomorrow starts our period of prayer and fasting. This is an important thing for all of us and I am looking to God to really touch our lives in a powerful way, that there might be a release of divine healing and life as we pray together.

Wednesday 13 July 2005   145 days after diagnosis
Since I last entered in the journal, a lot has happened, not least of which was our season of prayer and fasting. This came about through the response of people in church wanting to pray for Lesley. In the end we held three days, with the majority of church responding and getting involved in some way. Much good came out of the time, and it led me to a greater desire to follow after Jesus.

Otherwise the past weeks have been filled with a mixture of hopes and fears; times when life has been better, followed by days when the darkness has crept over our souls. Learning how to respond to the darkness has, for me, been a real trial of faith; to walk in hope and trust when fear resides as a close neighbour has not always been easy. This week we are waiting for the results of Lesley's treatment. We should meet with the consultant over the next ten days, and so this is a time of quiet trust and confidence in the God who is able to save us completely.

Charlotte has spent her first few hours at school over the past week – a big step in her little life, and we pray for her that she will settle quickly into this new environment, making friends and growing in confidence.

Discussions with the Church Council have led to the decision for me to take off the whole of August as a complete break. I just need to plan to use the time wisely, and benefit from it as a family to the maximum. We are planning to take at least a couple of weeks away.

Heavenly Father,
I commit this day to you. I thank you for our relationship together, and once again choose to follow after your ways in my life. Lead me today, Father, through the decisions of my life so that all my actions would honour you. I pray for Lesley, that today she would know your peace, power and healing in her body. Grant her your grace, Lord, and bring strength to her for this day. Keep her in your peace as she waits for the result of the scans, and fill her with hope and confidence for the future.
Amen.

Wednesday 17 August 2005
Well, I'm back again to the diary. Another month has passed, and I'm halfway through my extended leave. We've just got back from a week away in Cornwall, which was really nice. It was good to be away, just the three of us spending time pottering and visiting different things. The weather was great, which for Cornwall has to be a bonus!

A few weeks ago we got the results of Lesley's scans. They give a mixed picture – no progression and no regression, which leaves the consultants in a quandary; the positive side, of course, no progression; the negative, no regression. We had a further meeting this week, the outcome of which is to wait on a further scan in about a month. Meanwhile, the consultant will discuss the surgery option with his colleague, and we will talk about this next week. Lesley's is such an unusual case that the consultant is in uncharted water, not having any strong protocols to work from, which makes each step a difficult one.

Understandably, Lesley's feelings are mixed, compounded further by a greater intensity in the feelings in her face. Symptoms are something that the consultant will want to know about – our prayers are for them to calm over the next few days.

Heavenly Father,
I hold Lesley up before you again today. Please intervene in her life and bring restoration and peace into her heart. Show us a sign of your mercy and healing grace which we truly need from you. And extend your love towards her and us as a family.

May this tumour show signs of shrinkage over the next month; I pray for this in the name of Jesus. I ask, Lord, that next time a scan is taken shrinkage will be evident, a sign that this treatment and our prayers have been at work within her life and body.
Hear my prayer, Father.
Amen.

Tuesday 8 November 2005
I can see that I've been somewhat straying from my prayer diary. I guess there have been times when I've just not bothered to make an entry, and other times when I've sat quietly and prayed instead – other times when I've just missed doing it.

So where are we up to at present? Well, for the record, we said goodbye to our church elder, Graham Dobson and his wife Joyce two weeks back. It was a tough day and I was true to form, crying through a lot of the service. Goodness knows what people really thought, but at least they were kind to my face! It is a significant milestone for Charis[13] and us, since it marks a ten-year period in all of our lives. They've now relocated over to Matlock in Derbyshire – of course we will keep in touch as friends, but that eldership connection has now passed. I'm not over-anxious by the thought; what's more important at this stage is gathering more people around us who will help to push the vision of Charis forward, and it's good to see some of the younger adults taking on responsibility. Neil Fearn also joined us on staff in September. Neil is a great guy and I look forward to working with him over the next few years. He's on an initial two-year contract, and we will see how things progress from there.

As for our own lives, I'm so pleased that Lesley is feeling considerably better in herself. She's certainly more active, and we continue to pray for God to be at work in her body. We are waiting for news about a PET[14] scan they will perform to help diagnose more accurately what's taking place in her body. The purpose of this is to help get a true understanding of the mass that's been treated, to ensure it's no longer a viable tumour. Our prayers are therefore focused on this.

Charlotte continues in part-time school and is doing really well. We're really pleased, since we desperately wanted her to settle into school well, especially after the difficult time she had at nursery. Tonight, we will attend a parents meeting to see what class she will be in when she goes full-time in January.

And so to prayer:

Heavenly Father,

I pray for Lesley's continued well-being, and ask that strength would continue to be imparted to her. Strengthen her, Lord, and by your power cause this tumour to shrink and disappear. I ask, Father, that we would see this powerful act in Lesley's life – enable us to see the miracle through the journey and testify to your grace and power in our lives. I pray over her whole body for grace, love and healing to be released. May your glory shine through her life.

I pray too for Charis and all that we are about. Help us, Lord, to move forward. I pray for new people to come along to our gatherings, and thank you for those who have done so far. May your favour be revealed in us, Lord, as we seek to shine for you.

I pray for wisdom in leading this church and making the right decisions for the future. I also ask you for greater financial resources and more gifted people to join us in the Charis vision.

Help me, Father, to order my day right and to give myself over to those things you'd have me do. Enable me, Lord, to make good decisions with my time and sow my gifts into the cause of your kingdom.

Amen.

Wednesday 28 December 2005

Since I last wrote we've had two momentous things occur – my fortieth birthday, and secondly, the great news regarding Lesley. The recent PET scan she under-took has shown there are no living cancer cells remaining in the mass. This is fantastic news and a wonderful way to end the year. There is still concern that the mass remains, but nevertheless even the consultant smiled when he told us the news. I wrote afterwards to family and friends the following email:

Hi friends,

I'm sure that you will be delighted with us to hear the truly good news that we received during our recent visit to Lesley's consultant. He was able to confirm that the latest scan that was undertaken to determine whether there were active cancer cells in the tumour has read negative. The consultant viewed this as really encouraging. However, there is still concern that the tumour has not shown signs of shrinkage, which is what's expected as a result of treatment. A decision has been agreed that no further biopsy will be taken, and she will now undertake ongoing further assessment on the basis of clinical observation and MRI scans, the next of which will happen next February. This, after over eighteen months of intensive investigation and treatment, is a huge step forward for us, and one for which we truly thank God.

Thank you for your concern and prayers . . . we continue to value them, and especially that the tumour area would shrink and that Lesley would feel improvement in the facial nerves and muscle and eye that have suffered so much as a result of both the tumour and treatment for it.

Blessings to you all
Stephen and Lesley

And so such news led to a peaceful Christmas, which was a change from our feelings the previous year, when we were anticipating the biopsy that Lesley underwent in January.

It was whilst waiting for the results that we received a card from Gareth and Leanne Morgan from Newark. Along with a cheque for £40 was a quotation from Psalm 126: "Those who sow in tears will reap with songs of joy. He who goes out weeping, carrying seed to sow, will return with songs of joy, carrying sheaves with him' (vv. 5,6).

Even those of us who have professed to have walked the Christian pathway for many years still reveal our vulnerabilities during the difficult seasons of life. Trying to hear God's voice is a key to that journey, but discerning it with clarity is a patient and tested road. So when Scripture arrives through the door, we rightly take heart from the comfort it brings as the still small voice of God whispers 'it is well' to a troubled soul. You will understand my pleasure, then, to hear the verses quoted during prayer with my co-workers at Charis, and my heart was once more gladly warmed as I was further reminded that the God I love and serve is not silent.

Friday 30 December 2005
We visited our friends Graham and Joyce Dobson yesterday in their new home in Matlock. It was a great time, but reminded me of the year we've just been through; the turmoil, difficulties, farewells and goodbyes which have been part of the past twelve months. I always knew that 2005 was set to be a hard year, since many of the major issues were framed prior to it starting, and I'm glad to be at the end still in one piece!

Certainly the year changed me and I'm a different person from when we entered 2005. The journey from faithfulness to courage has certainly been stretched and challenged. As I enter my forties I can write with conviction about my love for God and desire to serve him. And the more I read, observe, learn and experience only serves to deepen that conviction. So the New Year will send me forth with a renewed commitment to make my time count for God, and to engage more fully with the generation I serve in communicating the ageless truth of Christ.

Heavenly Father,

I come to you today and thank you for your love and faithfulness during the past year. Thank you for your presence during the difficulties, and for your love upholding us through our fears. Help me to walk humbly before you, trusting you with my whole life and knowing that you are working for our good!

Empower me, Father, to wage war against the enemy and to live fully in the victory of Jesus on the cross. Help me to live in your Spirit and to discern his leanings in my life, family and ministry.

Help me, Lord, to know you better in the coming year, to respond more promptly to your voice, and to walk with greater boldness and confidence.

I pray for Lesley, that her strength would grow as the days pass and her quality of life would improve. Help her to gain recovery in her taste and smell, and develop a deeper sense of quality in her life. Thank you for your work of preservation over this year, for upholding her and enabling her to be strong. Thank you for healing, Lord.

Amen.

Chapter Three 2006

The Long Road Ahead

Think how you have instructed many,
how you have strengthened feeble hands.
Your words have supported those who stumbled;
you have strengthened faltering knees.
But now trouble comes to you, and you are discouraged;
it strikes you, and you are dismayed.
Should not your piety be your confidence
and your blameless ways your hope?

Job 4:3–6

Wednesday 1 February 2006
I nominated this as a reading week, but so far seem to have done little reading, although I have just about finished Donald Miller's book, *Blue Like Jazz*. What a great writer he is – realism essays is how he terms them, and I understand why; quite refreshing.

We're well on target for setting in place a budget for Charis for 2006, and a lot of my time has been absorbed with thinking and working that through. Laying things out in respect of the year has been a really positive exercise and I will certainly work like this much more in the future – planning realistic goals is so liberating. Of course, we now need to achieve them – but that's the fun bit, sort of . . .

Lesley is having a better time with her health, despite the fact she's had a nasty eye infection for the past week or so, but it is improving. She's also been approached by Fernwood Infant School to consider going in as a classroom assistant for a full term. After consideration she has decided to take it on – two days a week. She loves this type of work, and I'm sure it can only do her good. She will start after Easter.

Charlotte is now full-time at Fernwood Infant School in Class 10 with Mrs Artis. She's struggling a bit, but hopefully things will improve. We've had some tears and outbursts about not wanting to go to school. Apparently it's all to do with lunchtimes . . . We've switched her to sandwiches which seems to have helped. Cute little ham sandwiches in her box, along with sliced cucumber, a biscuit and smoothie. She's 5 now, and growing up.

The idea of the reading week is to set time aside to catch up with reading and study, to stop a little and think, pray and reflect. I've set three aside for 2006. Hopefully I'll get better and learn to make the most of the opportunity. I know it's important to have these times, seasons to set aside and reflect more on life and direction.

Heavenly Father,
I thank you for the opportunity to sit and reflect, to take time to think about life and relationships and ministry. Help me, Lord, to get the most I can out of these opportunities for growth and development.

I pray too for Lesley and Charlotte. Give them more grace today, Lord. Strengthen Charlotte at school and give her courage to build new friendships. Bless Lesley too,

Lord. I pray for continued strength, and ask specifically that you would bring restoration to her taste and smell. I pray specifically for this, Father, that her senses would be restored and she would develop a higher quality of life.

Watch over us, Lord, for we need your help. I pray too for myself, for health, strength, wisdom and confidence. May I walk closely with you, Father, and know the power of your Spirit within me.

Amen.

Wednesday 24 May 2006   460 days after diagnosis

Our lives have been shattered since I last wrote. What we'd considered to be a regular check-up for the results of Lesley's scan has delivered terrible news – the tumour has shown signs of significant growth. It's difficult to express just how hard this news is.

Until you're in that position of sitting opposite a consultant who is about to deliver bad news it's hard to express how you feel. Numb is probably the best word. From then you simply absorb the information and the consequences. For a moment your mind starts to drift, rather like waking from a deep sleep and recalling a bad dream, but then the daunting reality sinks into your mind and into your soul; this is no dream.

I felt sick – physically sick.

I felt sick for the next ten days.

The consultant arranged for us to visit the clinical oncologist that afternoon. We were both crying as we sat waiting to see her, and some kind person looked upon our plight and led us to a private room so our tears could be shed in private. There is no escaping that level of anxiety and fear – you simply have to live through it and see where it takes you.

Personally, it doesn't take me long to connect with God in those circumstances – prayer seems to be the natural – maybe the only – response. Not that he appears close. But faith and Scripture teach about our response in the midst of such darkness – I have no intention of making any other.

Consolation and words seem so pathetic at times like this. How do you speak to the one you love when such a daunting threat hangs over their life? I'm really not sure. Death is such a threat, such a challenge and it brings with it such fear. Not even the fear of dying, but that of being robbed of what is yours. Years that should lie ahead for you, to watch your child grow up; years to spend playing, dreaming and working – fulfilling your purpose and living your dream – all potentially taken from you by the cruelty of this merciless disease.

The oncologist was nice, considerate, but honest. She'd rehearsed the conversation many times. People in our position are normally scared, fearful and desperate. We're no exception. Normality descends like a dense fog on a cold winter's day, leaving you fumbling around for direction and light.

Chemotherapy would be the next treatment option for Lesley. We already knew it wasn't curative from our conversations with Mr McMahon. Chemotherapy is never curative by itself; it has to be used in conjunction with either surgery or radiotherapy or both for cancer to be cured. Remission would be the best solution, and even that's not guaranteed.

We returned home numbed by our afternoon's conversations, carrying a large plastic container for Lesley's urine sample when she returns to start chemotherapy treatment. Several weeks lay between today and her admittance.

When the day arrived, I remember showering that morning with a deep sense of foreboding. I knew somehow

I was beginning to live with inevitability and it was slowly changing me. We said little as we drove up the motorway, each in our own thoughts and not quite sure where those thoughts were taking us. We arrived early and managed to get a space in the small car park, and before long were sent for a chest X-ray. (It's a precautionary measure to ensure no infections before the body is pounded with poison in an attempt to kill something even more lethal.) I remember sitting waiting for Lesley thinking, 'This is it, then. This is the beginning of the end and this is what it looks like, sitting in an X-ray department waiting for your wife to come out to start a terrible course of treatment that might lengthen her life but not cure her illness.' I remember pondering the point of it all, and feeling terribly guilty for fostering such thoughts. I remember quietly praying, but feeling like the ceiling was made of lead, like that which separated me from Lesley in her X-ray room. It all felt very dark that day, very dark and very lonely.

Before we'd arrived, Lesley had asked if she could have a side room rather than be on the main ward. Although they were not able to promise, she did get her own room, with a view over the main road outside. And so with all the checks done, bloods, X-rays and temperature she was connected up to an IV drip and flushed through with clean water before the toxic drugs were administered. The prescription was a cocktail of two, both of which come with a hideous list of potential side-effects, all of which was almost irrelevant when one considered the alternative.

Those next five days were timed like clockwork, and as one bag of chemotherapy[15] finished another started, as pints of fluorouracil and cisplatin were slowly released into the body. Altogether there would be thirty days of treatment delivered over six weeks with a month between each treatment to allow the body to recover. When I drove home that first night after Dave and Val arrived, I just broke down in the car, and had to pull over for a while to get my composure; there was a long road ahead.

Wednesday 29 June 2006
Today we return to Weston Park for Lesley's scan. This will tell us whether the treatment is having the desired effect on the tumour of either controlling or shrinking it.

I anointed Lesley with oil last night and prayed over her. It's taken some time to get back to a place of faith to be able to pray in such a way. It appears that at such times you really are dependent upon others to pray for you. Your own emotions are simply too close to the situation to get that level of breakthrough.

Meanwhile, we work at keeping busy and focused on other things. It's a blessing to be able to work and concentrate on other priorities. I finalised an offer on a flat in Clifton which a young family will occupy.

The Clifton Shop[16] has now been refitted and opened – it looks really great and, along with the appointment of a new manageress, we hope it will be even more effective over the coming months. We've renamed it 'Hope Charity Shop'.

Heavenly Father,
I pray for Lesley's health. Watch over her, Lord, and keep her safe. I especially pray for deliverance and healing for her. May this scan bring positive news. Please sustain us, Lord. We need your grace and mercy in our lives, but also your strength and power – in our weakness we fall upon you for help.
Thank you Lord.
Amen.

Thursday 27 July 2006

What is it about pressure that causes you to so easily lose perspective and devalue your own priorities? I've had a bad few days – a bad week actually . . . well, to be honest, over recent times I'm reckoning I've had a hard life. Life is hard, of course, and ours especially so, but does that give me an excuse for loss of perspective? Sometimes I can let myself off the hook – give myself a breather – but I'm going to need to be careful, otherwise I could end up all mixed up.

Last night I gave time to watching stuff I ought not to – it really does me no good, but I was low – I hope not depressed but, well . . . whatever, the outcome is the same. I really don't want to live in that way. I desire to be a better husband, father, leader and disciple.

Today I will focus again on what is important, work within clearer parameters and seek to commit to doing what is right. So help me God!
Amen.

Monday 30 October 2006   619 days after diagnosis

Another trip to the consultant, the purpose to consolidate the bad news he'd delivered two weeks earlier. The tumour which had reduced by 30 per cent after the initial three rounds of chemo has, after the six month scan, shown signs of growth – this time beyond the blood line barrier and into the bottom side of the brain.

After such a long journey you anticipate bad news can't get any worse, only to discover that it can. We both took the news in a 'matter of fact' fashion; I reckon this is what sustained pressure does to you – it numbs the pain, and I'm not sure if that's good or not.

We're now due back next week to see a professor of oncology offering specialist treatment in the area of the brain.

Prior to our latest visit, Lesley and I had spoken at some length about what all of this means. Without some form of miracle it now appears clearer than ever that Lesley's life will be cut short. A miracle is the only way out at this stage – and they seem to be in short supply.

In response to the 'miracle' we went for prayer to a Craig Marsh healing meeting at the Christian Centre. It was a good night, listening to a man who has received his miracle and now travels the world praying for others to receive theirs. We know where we stand and what we believe and hope for. Lesley went for prayer – and managed to keep her wig on! The prayer was strong and passionate with many of the leaders at the Christian Centre gathering round us.

It's good to take these opportunities for prayer, since when you live in the situation we are faced with you become unsure where to take your prayers . . . I feel somewhat 'prayed up', not really knowing what to say any more – concerned that my repetition may be more detrimental to Lesley than helpful. My prayers for her have therefore taken a more personal slant over recent months. I think I may be suffering from prayer fatigue.

Lord, I believe – but please help me in my unbelief.

Tuesday 31 October 2006
This morning I read, 'Why are you downcast, O my soul? Why so disturbed within me? Put your hope in God, for I will yet praise him, my Saviour and my God.'[17]

It seemed appropriate.

Wednesday 1 November 2006
I've had two conversations thus far today – both surround Lesley's health. Both are from well meaning and good friends, and I don't mind speaking with them. In

fact, it's good to have people showing such high level of concern.

I sometimes wonder at what stage in a situation like ours you switch from what you can change in it to what you should learn from it. Perhaps it's not so much a switch as a progression. The less likely it is to change, the more you look to see what you can learn. If that's the case, at some point I ought to be well educated!

Part of today's Bible reading included verses from Psalm 119:49,50: 'Remember your word to your servant, for you have given me hope. My comfort in my suffering is this: Your promise preserves my life.'

Heavenly Father,
May these words ring true of our situation. May your promise preserve our life. I pray over the news we received about Lesley's health. Father, help us to find the way forward in all of this. Help us to overcome the fear, to correctly measure our lives and to walk humbly and faithfully before you – even when we are unsure of all of those implications.

I pray for wisdom for the consultants and interventions of a divine nature to occur within Lesley's body. Help us, Lord, through our suffering, to find you.
Amen.

The words of the 'Serenity Prayer' by Reinhold Niehbuhr came to mind as I offered my own prayers today – this is the full version:

> God, grant me the serenity to accept the things I cannot change;
> courage to change the things I can; and
> the wisdom to know the difference.
> Living one day at a time;

enjoying one moment at a time;
accepting hardship as the pathway to peace.
Taking, as He did, this sinful world as it is, not as I
would have it.
Trusting that He will make all things right, if I surrender
to His will.
That I may be reasonably happy in this life,
and supremely happy with Him forever in the next.

Tuesday 7 November 2006
We met with Professor Robinson yesterday. It was a
planned visit to discuss further options for treatment on
Lesley's tumour, and having sat for well over an hour in
the waiting room, we went across to the consultation
room to meet him.

A man in his early sixties, Professor Robinson was
well versed in his field, and our first fifteen minutes
were spent covering Lesley's history to date. The significant gap between Lesley's original tumour and this new
cancer was displayed in her records. And then from
about three years back, things had changed dramatically, her file to date now thick with scans and more
scans, reports and investigations and consultations –
we'd spent many hours sitting in waiting rooms await-
ing our turn.

A short time later and we were discussing Lesley's latest scans and what further treatment options might be
available. We'd crossed a significant barrier in her
options earlier this year when she undertook first line
chemotherapy. The success in seeing a 30 per cent reduc-
tion in the overall tumour was great news, and we'd
undertaken the latest scans with the optimism that the
tumour was being held in abeyance. It was a serious
blow to be told it had broken through the blood line barrier to the brain and the disease had progressed – albeit

subtly – to a new level. That news, some three weeks earlier, had taken its toll on both our emotional states. Much of that night had been spent, through tears, discussing the future; a future which, in Lesley's heart, she knew she would not be a part of. It's difficult to disagree with her feelings – everything points towards a slow, difficult end to this disease. We've not discussed matters at the same depth since then – you simply can't keep visiting such a place. It's like having a blunt spade plunged into your stomach and slowly turned.

Since now we are looking at palliative care for Lesley, the pace at which she takes further treatment has lessened. Presently her symptoms are stable, her health relatively good – 'So why take drugs that will make you poorly?' was the consultant's advice. 'Better to enjoy a window of health, hold the drug options for later, and scan early in the New Year to see what's happening . . .' It seems like a reasonable approach when you consider all the options. Meanwhile, I will probably contact her old consultant Jeremy McMahon and talk about taking the second opinion we'd discussed in times past. At least doing something feels like a positive step.

As for me, the words of Psalm 139 are in my mind, 'even the darkness will not be dark to you . . . for darkness is as light to you' (v. 12). Well, the truth of those words needs to come into our experience, and that's where I rest my prayers.

Friday 1 December 2006

Some days I just feel like crying, and today is one of them. Lesley got up early to take Charlotte to school and when we came back she was tired. These days she normally lies in bed till later when she can bring herself to get up, but this morning she really made the effort since Charlotte was upset yesterday when she couldn't go with her. So when we got back home she laid on the settee with a bowl of porridge, and after a while drifted back off to sleep. I sat with her on the floor, working on the laptop till she nodded off. I think it was the postman who set me off this morning. He delivered a card from some friends who'd emigrated earlier in the year to Australia. It spoke about the wonderful new life they were creating for themselves – and that was it. The tranquillity of their life contrasted harshly with what I consider to be the brutality of our own, and I was gone. You may call it self-centredness, but I know the joy that is theirs will never be ours, and the contrast was too daunting not to be affected by it.

What with that, and then looking at Lesley sleeping and seeing the ongoing effects of this disease, slowly yet relentlessly having its way, one's left with a bleak and difficult prospect and once again tears become a comforting friend and my only relief. Even with faith, life is hard during these dark days.

Last week I contacted Jeremy McMahon to discuss the prospect of a second opinion on treatment options for Lesley. This is the email I sent to him, along with his reply:

Dear Jeremy
It's been some time since we last spoke so please excuse my further contact out of the blue. I thought I'd email in the first instance rather than call your mobile.

Lesley has now undergone her six month chemo course which she finished in September. The initial three month scan showed a 30 per cent shrinkage in the overall mass which we took, in the circumstances, as measured good news – as you know only too well, everything is 'measured' in these situations. A further scan at the end of the treatment was not so kind; it showed that the overall shrinkage had remained, however progression through the blood brain barrier and into a small part of the brain was now evident on the scan (approx 1 cm. x 1.5 cm.). I'd not realized that the blood brain barrier was something that chemo found hard to penetrate and thus (in my layman's mind) it could be that although the treatment had shown effect to the majority of the tumour, it was not as effective in that area.

Initially, Dr Purohit referred Lesley back to Mr Ward and conversations were undertaken with the larger skull based team which included Mr Carroll. The question poised was: had the tumour shrunk sufficiently for surgery to come back into the equation? Apparently not, but from our long conversations with you in the past we're not too surprised. That the tumour remain 'contained' at 30 per cent was our hope.

We've now been referred to Professor Robinson at oncology – I think they want to reassure us that we've spoken with every possible consultant within this field! As you know, we're working with palliative chemotherapy, and they do have one or two further drugs for Lesley to try – with a potential new one coming to clinical trials in the 'not too distant future'. We've agreed with Mr Robinson to leave any further treatment till after Christmas, since Lesley's health is 'good' at present and she really has no further symptoms than she did, say, twelve months ago – albeit now she has her taste and smell back, which is good.

We spoke about second opinions with him, and he was keen that we should pursue them – if only from the perspective of personal empowerment in the situation. I discover that, in our position, you must continually examine options and look into alternatives, even if they appear remote.

With this in mind we both discussed contacting yourself for a little help. Several things come to mind.

1. Would it be possible for you to contact Dr Robinson and speak with him? I understand you know him from your time at Sheffield. In this way he'd bring you up to speed with the technical data on Lesley, and I wondered if between the two of you, you could suggest a good place or person to seek a second opinion from. I know in times past you spoke with a colleague in London whom you'd suggested would be pleased to see us. Would that still be appropriate, or in light of the present situation, would a different type of consultant be preferable?

2. Secondly, I came across an interesting article in the papers over the weekend for a new kind of delivery system for tumours within the brain. It appears it is still in its infancy and remains to be taken to clinical trials on humans so I'm not sure how long all that takes, but it did seem like a treatment option which, if it came available, could be considered? The article I read can be found at: www.eurekalert.org/pub_releases/2006-11/uomh-uru111406.php. I wondered if you were familiar with the concept? I've not abandoned myself to hours of intense research on the Internet, but when you hear of things, you can't help but check it out.

When you get the chance, perhaps you could let us know your thoughts. We'd be happy to call you . . . but only at your convenience.

With best regards
Stephen and Lesley Hackney

Jeremy replied the same day:

Dear Stephen,
Thank you for the email and an update on Lesley's progress. Thank you also for the link to the interesting research on iron oxide particles as a carrier for drugs. We have been interested in looking at its use diagnostically

for the detection of cancer in lymph glands, but had not thought of it as a delivery system for drugs. Unfortunately it does not look as if the drug has got into the clinical trial arena as yet. I will keep my ear to the ground at meetings and in journals and if I come across any trials of novel treatments will be sure to let you know.

I had spoken to Sean Ward and Tom Carroll two weeks ago and we talked about Lesley so I was aware of the situation. Tom took the view that it would be impossible to achieve a meaningful surgical removal of the tumour and I think he is right. Furthermore the risks of trying would be high. There is absolutely no reason why you should not get further opinions and the key is to get the right opinion. I think David Howard in London would be good and I would be very happy to get John Crowther and Bill Taylor from the skull base team up here to give their view. They are also very good. I will telephone Martin Robinson this week and get back to you.

Jeremy

Chapter Four 2007

Changes and Challenges

> We were under great pressure, far beyond our ability to endure, so that we despaired even of life. Indeed, in our hearts we felt the sentence of death. But this happened that we might not rely on ourselves but on God, who raises the dead. He has delivered us from such a deadly peril, and he will deliver us. On him we have set our hope that he will continue to deliver us, as you help us by your prayers. Then many will give thanks on our behalf for the gracious favour granted us in answer to the prayers of many.
>
> 2 Corinthians 1:8–11

Monday 1 January 2007

Out with the old and in with the new. Both Lesley and Charlotte are in bed, snuggled up together, and so I thought I'd take the opportunity to make my first entry of the New Year.

Earlier at church, the ministry I led became very emotional, with many tears shed both on my part as well as other people's. The result was that people offered prayers on our behalf. I took the opportunity to pray specifically for Lesley and to stand against the disease and tumour in her head. This was an important moment, and I wanted to ensure I marked it in my diary. On Tuesday we will attend the hospital for Lesley's next scan – it will be an important one and the first since she was also prayed for at the Christian Centre Healing Mission.

Monday 15 January 2007
Late last week Lesley told me how she felt God would speak to her on New Year's Day. I'd given a sermon I felt quickened to me during a session earlier that week reading 2 Corinthians. It's very powerful and, although you have to be careful with both context and interpretation, I did feel it spoke to us – on hearing, Lesley did too. What to make of all these things is still unclear, but it's still a real comfort to receive them . . .

We went to get the results today, and the scan showed further signs of 'slight' progression. Any progression is not good, regardless of how slight, but in times past the word has been 'significant growth', so 'slight' has to be better. This second scan report made no reference to the previous, when it was said the tumour had broken through the blood brain barrier. We asked the consultants to review this and get back with some further information; this information would provide the basis upon which we will make a decision about her next treatment option. Treatment options are getting less so we need some wisdom as to how and when to make the decision.

It's a very strange experience sitting with people discussing your wife's health, or lack of it, discussing options which are no longer curative, but simply seeking to hold the cancer at bay. It's all so clinical and detached; it must be the number of times we've been there and discussed it that numbs you to the realities you face. Without a miracle, Lesley's life will be taken by this disease – I don't know when, but it will be taken. Can God break through for us? One must hope and pray.

Sunday 18 February 2007
I stayed up tonight to finish watching the movie *Gladiator* and cried at the end of it. The story of revenge set against the backdrop of his murdered wife and son was hard to take. He believed that death would finally reunite them, and after he wrought revenge on the corrupt emperor by taking his life in the Coliseum, he died from his wounds and was, according to the film, united in death. It was a painful thing to watch, and I spent some time in silent screams and tears at the end of it as I contemplated our own fate.

I'm not sure what it does to you going through what we are experiencing. I know that eventually it starts to mess with your head. Normality is a far distant memory now, and many are the times I have longed for it; for times when the last thought at night and the first in the morning is not connected to my wife's illness and the implications of that upon us all. Times when we could plan for a holiday, or a change that might be the predominant thought in the mind, rather than what we face. I've finally finished the dining room, which at least brings a little pleasure, but it all feels so trivial and unimportant in the light of this dark shadow that looms over us. The things that would bring pleasure and normality to most families simply bring sedation to us. It masks the reality and provides escapism if only for a moment.

Some people talk about life being dreadful – if by that they mean it is full of dread then I fear I may be able to identify with them. You never really believe your life will turn so terrible when you feel so relatively young.

But it does for some – and we are amongst them, and when I consider it at its worst, I wonder how we will get through.

As I write, Charlotte still has no comprehension of the depth of the issue going on around her. We've worked hard at keeping things stable and secure and will continue this way for some time yet. Things of course will change. May God help us when they do.

Sometimes I wonder how I should face Lesley's illness in light of faith – and ministry. Prayers for healing – for coping . . . Must stop there; I can hear Charlotte crying.

Sunday 9 March 2007
Like an idiot, read Justin Toper – 'Your Date with Destiny' – in *Express* Supplement.
Never read it before and will never read it again. It said something about life's greatest pleasures being on offer now . . . The world is full of crap!

Saturday 17 March 2007
This week saw some change in Lesley's condition. She suffered some difficult problems in her head. A week last Wednesday she called me quickly after tea, and in the bathroom I saw something of the distress that this new condition is creating for her. A 'darkness' comes, over which she has no control. After it has passed she is left feeling sick and with a head pain. It's concerning.

This experience was repeated a week later, and then this Thursday she suffered six such sensations through the course of the day. She called me at work on Thursday morning, and I came rushing home to find her in bed, exhausted and scared by the experience. The same thing happened in the evening when I had popped out for an hour.

Friday she had no problems. She says her face has no pain and feels quite strong. As a result she lay on the other side of her face in bed, which led to a lot of stuff coming out of her ear.

Lesley says something has changed this week – but she is not sure whether it is for the better or worse. Neither am I! Time will tell.

What is for certain is that this type of life begins to mess with your head, heart and emotions. I feel vulnerable – everything in my life revolves round working out the call of God, and yet I feel it could all fall round me. If it did then I would be left with nothing – no wife, no job, no money, no career and no prospect – what joy!

Tuesday 20 March 2007   760 days after diagnosis
Chaos. Sometimes life is just too hard to think about.
It's Lesley's birthday – she is 36 today. Of course she wonders whether she will get to 37, and so do I. Last night she said how she felt she was going through a year of last things: last birthday, Christmas, summer etc. How hard is that? I really don't know what to say to her – I don't what to say to myself – and no one else seems to know either.

I'm really not sure where I am at with all of this; as I sit here today and look at her picture I feel the pain of loss – and that's before she's gone. Am I going mad?

She slept in again this morning and I went quietly and looked at her. It's horrible – a dreadful thing to look at someone you love and imagine the disease inside slowly having its nasty way, and there is nothing – absolutely nothing – you can do about it apart from watch, pray and wait.

And then there is Charlotte. What the hell am I going to say to her? When is the right time to speak about her mummy's illness? We went shopping for her mum on

Saturday and bought some things for her birthday and Mother's Day. A nice jacket and top from Next, along with some chocolates from Hotel Chocolat. We stopped off at Starbucks for some hot chocolate to share, and talked and laughed while we shared a big chocolate cookie.

A few days earlier, she wrote her own card for her mum: 'To mummy, I will always love you and happy birthday.'

I cry for her – it is nothing short of heartbreaking to imagine your child having to grow up without her mum. I once read that losing a parent to death is better than losing them to divorce. I'm not so sure. At least in divorce the child gets to keep both parents.

There seems little sanctuary in what we face in illness. The disease carries both of you in two separate directions: one towards dying – the other to life without their partner. It was never meant to go this way. Where is the happy ever after? Not for us, I fear.

Life is a double-edged sword; in one sense you are brought closer in disease, in another you are pulled further apart. You often withdraw for space by yourself; a time to think, cry and think a bit more. You break down, pull yourself back together and go out to answer the millionth person who asks the same tired question: 'How are you?'

It's very weird to arrive in a place where you can no longer comfort each other's fears because you know you won't be able to face them together. For nearly twenty years you have walked through each situation and faced every crisis as a couple. Looked at every obstacle – and there have been many – and said, 'Come on, we can get through this together.' But what when you face separation brought on by disease . . . What do you say to each other then? Not much. In fact, presence substitutes for words. You simply sit and hold each other – allow them to cry and then move away and give that person space to deal with what it means to come to terms with facing the issue alone – very alone.

Then, of course, there's the issue of other people . . . how much do you say – what should be the topic of conversation?

My head is far too full of things to spill it easily over someone else. In fact, maybe no one should ever know what goes on inside your head at times like these. What can anyone ever do? What can they say that might remotely help?

Who can remove my guilt, dissolve my fear and take away my anxieties? And what about those thoughts of life moving on without her? Of meeting someone else? What does that mean – how can it be right, and yet how can you not? The guilt. The sadness. It's all in there and perhaps that is the best place for it.

Then, of course, there is the anger – the harsh anger of injustice but also selfishness. I'm glad none of us choose our end, since I don't know which I would take. To go out, get knocked down in one day has its advantages – it's all over quickly. With what we face, the pain is exacerbated. You start to let go but need to hold on. The powerlessness – oh, the terrible powerlessness.

In the midst of all this chaos I will gird myself to ensure I do the very best for Charlotte. Her life matters more than anyone else in this sorry saga.

God, please help me to protect Charlotte through everything she will have to endure as a small child. She is so innocent, lovely, and pure – so young to have to endure such loss. Yet her life is to be irrevocably changed. Please God, help me to limit the damage in her mind, spirit and emotions.

Amen.

I'm not sure when grief kicks in for someone you love. For me, it felt like it started over four years ago when this dark cloud fell on us. It is a storm cloud we have endured for those years, which sometimes leaves me numb, whilst at other times I seek to hide it amongst the activity of life. Work has become the drug taken to remove the pain by occupying my mind with other things.

Thursday 31 May 2007
I wish I could find space to start a diary entry on a positive note, but it won't be today.

I can't begin to start to bring my entries up to date, and it's over two months since I last wrote. In the meantime, Lesley has had some good days and plenty of bad ones. She has endured many strange and weird happenings in her head which are hard for her to explain – but very distressing for her to endure and for me to witness. We kept them private for quite some time, but more recently spoke to her mum about them.

This week we have been busy with the Love Clifton[18] event, but in the midst of it Lesley has endured a terrible week emotionally and physically. I'm not sure that I help in those situations; even when I try to, my fear is I fall far short. Tonight she sat quiet for most of the evening, not talking and me not knowing how to talk. How do you get to that place after twenty years of being together: she not talking and me not daring to, lest I raise issues I can't resolve and make the situation worse?

Last night was also terrible. Lesley felt dreadful, had no energy and asked me whether I thought it was in her head. I responded that it could be, to which she burst into tears, broke down and has hardly spoken to me since. Who can blame her? What a bastard I am. How do I do this? How do I help her? What is help for

Lesley? I feel drained, exhausted and powerless. God help us.

At present, I'm sitting on my own downstairs and just finished watching *Question Time*. Lesley has gone to bed – I need to go and join her.

Wednesday 18 July 2007
I've just got off the phone from speaking with my friend Andrew Belfield. What a great support he has been to me over these hard times. We spoke a lot and prayed and cried over the phone. The things grown-up blokes do! It helped. I shared some of my personal challenges, and issues Lesley and I are facing at present. They are all my fault. I won't commit them to print.

Lesley and I had a terrible night. On the back of her prompting, I spoke about some of my feelings – they relate to other people. I can't go there.

I fear I am becoming part of the problem – making Lesley's plight worse and not better. I must turn this situation round. May God give me strength.

We went to see the consultant on Monday to talk about the results of the scan. It's not good news. The tumour continues to grow. It is progressing in each direction into her jaw, sinus cavity, eye socket and brain. They don't want to run any further scans, simply monitor her condition symptomatically. 'Why take scans when it only gives us bad news that we have no power to change?' was the consultant's rationale. I think it's standard protocol. A further line of chemo is on offer and she needs to consider when and if to take it. Such impossible decisions.

Friday 27 July 2007   889 days after diagnosis
It all blew off today. I'm not too sure where it all goes from here. Lesley has left me and gone to her parents – I

can hardly blame her. I've held the conviction that whenever a relationship goes wrong it is always the man's fault, and this is no exception. It is all my fault. I'd previously confessed to Lesley that I had enjoyed conversations with another woman and the thoughts of those conversations ran round in my head. It was not good. I had brought them under a certain amount of control but I did ponder on them. Worse still, I had fed them. Meeting her meant I could build a friendship, and I saw her maybe once or twice a week for five or ten minutes at a time – sometimes longer, but not often.

I'd sent her a few texts over the months, about half a dozen or so. I'd previously told Lesley about having swapped mobile numbers when we spoke about these matters. It's a long story of how you get into these things. It goes something like this. The only danger with writing to justify your actions is that you apportion blame by default – otherwise there can be no justification for those actions. I don't wish to apportion blame – I am the one to blame, no excuses. I'm a big boy now.

Here goes.

I love Lesley, and still love her. Period. So how can I live with thoughts of the future – a future with a different person? I can't. They torment me. The torment simply adds to the brokenness I already feel. The brokenness I live with every day. That can't be changed.

Life changes us. It has certainly changed me. I'm much more sceptical now, harder to life and what it might bring. Sadly, I'm also more selfish. I live in the process of self-preservation. I'm also grieving for a love that I am losing and will lose. I'm scared. Scared of that prospect, and I look for hope – sometimes, living beyond the present, I allow my emotions and thoughts to fast track forward one, two, or even three years. I go to a time when Lesley will no longer be with me and I imagine that life.

What it will be like, how we will cope. What it will mean
to me, Charlotte and our parents. I think possessively
about my life. It is a dangerous place to live. An unreal
world of fantasy and hype, yet tinged with the fact that
this fantasy will one day, in some form, become my new
reality. That's where it all starts.

To get there takes time – a long time, in fact. It comes
as a culmination of events, experiences and conversations. Meetings with consultants, doctors, going for
scans and more scans, and then taking the news. Bang,
and then bang again. Bad news . . . it's all bad news.

Eventually, bad news affects you. It affects how you
feel about yourself and those around you. It affects how
you feel about the present and the future. It doesn't happen all at once. It takes time. Time and thought. I've had
my share of both.

When Lesley's treatment didn't work first time round
it was bad news – see, there it is again. That was on top
of the bad news of discovering the cancer in the first
place. I thought about that – a lot. Truthfully, I'd been
thinking about it a long time before then. My mind
became obsessed with it. I'd drift away in meetings
thinking about it, or find myself daydreaming at my
desk whilst sitting in my office which I'd built some
years earlier . . . whilst I'd been building it, my mind was
also thinking about Lesley – and losing her. Those
thoughts have lived in my head every waking hour for
over four years. There is never a break from them.
Never. I don't want to complain too much, but this is the
only means I have to express myself.

Over time, those thoughts change you. You don't
want them or wish them too. They just do. I don't know
whether this process is the same for everyone, but it's
how it works in me. I start to dwell on the future. I cry a
lot. Then I stop. Then cry some more. It's alright; don't

feel sorry for me; crying helps. I cry in all sorts of places and different times. Sometimes I will look at the picture at the bottom of our stairs of Lesley sitting with Charlotte on her first day at school. It catches my eye – I cry. Other times, late at night when everyone is in bed, I will go over to our small wedding picture and look at it. I cry, or sob. The only difference is to do with intensity. Many times I have gone to Lesley in the morning, looked at her sleeping and stared at her face, the eye that's damaged and the gaunt expression. I go away to cry.

My summer house has become a haven for my tears; a place to hide, weep, sob, and pour out my heart to God. I usually don't know what to say because I've said it so many times over the past few years. I never thought you could find comfort in tears. I wish I'd never had to find that out.

Sometimes I will drive in the car and cry. Maybe just a simple thought comes to mind, or a song will come on the radio. You never quite know where and by what your emotions will be triggered.

Then you stop crying, and the relief that crying brings hardens you to the reality of what you face. You harden to your lot. You encase yourself in steel and determine not to be crushed. You rise up. It's a reaction. It's not even intentional. It happens. Maybe that is just me, the way I do things.

I go on. I must go on. I speak to myself. I remind myself that I cannot change what cannot be changed. I'm strong and the journey begins. It is not a journey that I have chosen, but one that's been forced upon me. I am a happily married man. I love Lesley and Charlotte. I wanted to have another baby, to enjoy holidays together, to travel and enjoy new experiences. I wanted a home that was full of fun and laughter, joy and happiness. I wanted this for me, for us – for my family. And then this. It will not be. Smashed.

My instincts rise. I will build it again. The journey begins. It's only in my head – not even my heart. I try to imagine a future without Lesley, with – yes – someone else. There is no person there. No attachment. Until, a glance here and a look there causes me to consider a possibility. It is madness; sheer stupidity. I'm running scared. Scared of what I will lose. Through fear and insecurity I try to imagine if I could get what I have now anywhere else. It is a journey I cannot travel but my mind takes me there. I take charge of my mind. I fail. Then I succeed. Then fail again. I am exhausted.

A tender moment, a simple thought and silent wish, a moment's vulnerability and I am back. Here is Lesley and our life and love together. However could I live without her? I am dying inside. Someone help me, please.

The process begins again and the tears start to flow.

It's been like this for a long time now. In fact, it feels like longer than it is. Sometimes I look at the picture of Lesley I keep in my tray; a picture from when we lived in our first home at Church Lane. She looks beautiful, with neck-length golden hair and a radiant smile. It's one of my favourite pictures of her – that, and the one taken in Gran Canaria when her hair was wet and she had a towel wrapped around her bikini. It's really sexy. I cannot imagine my life without this woman. But then I have to – and this is the sorry state of my mind. The place I am in. I hate it. I hate everything about it.

Saturday 28 July 2007
I went to see John Pettifor last night, which really helped. I spoke about what had happened and showed him the texts I had sent. I spoke with him again today.

He said I was 'guilty of being a prat' by letting my imagination get carried away, but nothing more than that. He has empathy to our plight and extends his grace through his judgements. I hope he is right.

I also went to see my mum and dad and spoke to them. They were obviously distressed by what I told them about Lesley and me. Understandably they were really upset – especially in the circumstances . . . We spoke at some length and then I travelled home.

I'm going to get something to eat and then off to bed.

Sunday 29 July 2007

Lesley and Charlotte are still at her parents' house and have gone out for the afternoon. I spoke with Lesley briefly this morning. She said she would ring later and I will take some clothes over for them both. I'd planned to go earlier in the day, but now it will have to be this evening.

I spent the morning walking in the park, eating a bacon sandwich for lunch and reading the Sunday paper this afternoon. I came across an article for a drug that has been used in brain tumours – I'm going to look it up on the net.

I pray I can sort this sorry mess out with Lesley, that it is seen for what it is and not more. I am so sorry to have put this on her; I can't believe I have. Why didn't I just tell her about the conversations? I mean, I had some fantasy idea about the future, but the conversations were just that – conversations in the context of friendship. I've been a fool.

In my conversation yesterday, Lesley told me about the difference between the love she feels at her parents and the lack of it with me, and that she must protect herself now. She is a selfless person so that will be a first. But I do love her. If only people knew what this is like.

How could I ever explain how I feel? She went on to tell me about how I lacked love during the time she had chemotherapy. I would turn up, spend an hour or so with her from 12 till 1 p.m., go off for a couple of hours and come back about 3 p.m. and stay till about 7 p.m. when her parents arrived. This would be my normal practice over the five days she was in, for the six weeks of treatment. She hated it, I hated it. I remember how she pulled the table round her, the order in which she placed the drinks and tablets. How it all needed to be just right. There was a measure of precision and security attached to it. It was if she was being institutionalized in that place, her life ordered by the directions of others. A world apart from who she was, she was now becoming someone else. I was just slowly dying inside.

I dreaded those weeks and the times leading up to them. Lesley hated every part of it and yet faced it with courage and grace. It was so cruel. The arrival meant a long wait in admissions on the top floor of a sixties-built hospital. We'd arrive from the squeaky lift and sit in a large, empty room with chairs set out in circles. Everyone was always older than us – or it certainly appeared that way. There was a small portable television in one corner, with an internal aerial that meant you got a fuzzy picture and just one channel to choose from. The first day of Lesley's treatment was the Queen's Fiftieth Anniversary Celebrations, and we watched some of it whilst waiting to be called in by the doctor.

Afterwards, we were sent back to the waiting room until it was time to go down to the ward. Once on the ward, Lesley would stay there for five whole days. She never left the ward, never went to the day room or the conservatory. She would lie there, only getting off the bed to go to wash and use the toilet. This is how it was during every visit; nothing ever changed.

These were some of the most difficult days in our marriage. My actions left Lesley traumatized and me ashamed. The fact that I'd covered up something that I needn't have done left her understandably suspicious. She already felt my coldness at times and resentment towards her illness and the way it impacted our lives in every way. The loss of intimacy and joy, the lack of sexual contact and slow erosion of the normality of life left it under huge strain. It was unlike anything we'd known. We had gone from a position of such strength and closeness to this deeply low point. I doubt that she ever really got over it or forgave me for my actions and I can't really blame her. We all pay a price for love, and it appeared to be costing both of us all we had. The only redemption at such a low point was the fact that what we'd had together was so special that it extended our tolerance towards each other far beyond normal boundaries.

Over the next few weeks we worked at making amends and putting things back together. We spent some time with Lesley's parents before going back home and preparing for a holiday in Bournemouth at the end of August. We didn't know at the time, but it would be her last visit to the coast, and we all enjoyed it enormously. Over the years we had spent many holidays there, and so found the familiarity strangely comforting. By now, the hospital had put Lesley on steroids which gave her an artificial boost. It was as if above-normal energy levels had resumed overnight, allowing her to get up much more easily in the morning – so much so that when it came to Charlotte's first day back at school, Lesley was able to accompany her; something she had not been able to do for many months.

Whilst in Bournemouth she was feeling much better, so much so that she began to wonder if something was happening to her by way of healing. I remember having a great yet painful conversation walking up the long hill to our hotel, holding hands and daring, if only for those moments, to imagine a life that included a physical miracle. Like me, Lesley often looked for healing out of faith and desperation, and it was difficult for anyone to believe that such a tiny tablet could account for the dramatic improvement in her symptoms; hence the reason for an increase in optimism. Whatever was happening, it not only affected her energy levels but also significantly reduced her pain, making the days more enjoyable in every way. It was like a miracle drug and we desired that it might be the start of a real miracle. We both remained open to the possibility – longed for it, even.

Over the next few weeks the physical changes were remarkable, but it did come at a cost in other ways. Not only was her body chasing, but her mind was too. Her personality was affected by the steroids, making her forceful and opinionated . . . not that she wasn't already opinionated, but now her opinions were supercharged and one challenged them at one's peril! We had several late night sessions when tensions were high and discussions strained, and they would go on into the early hours. I'd be longing to get to bed for some sleep, knowing I needed to be up in the morning to get Charlotte to school, but Lesley's mind was in overdrive and appeared to be at its sharpest when the rest of us were longing for sleep. Sometimes it was like the scene from a film set; all it needed was for her to yell out as I tried to retire to bed: 'Come down here and fight me like a man!' It made for some difficult weeks, yet outside of this tension it led to more normal days in the sense that we were able to get out and do things more easily. It all felt very strange; it was all very strange. This was Lesley, but not as I knew her. Little did we realize at the time that there was another price to be paid for being on such strong steroids: a lowering of the immunity system.

Thursday 11 October 2007 965 days after diagnosis
Lesley has been poorly over the past few days, so much so that I have been prompted to call her mum and she has come down to support us. Her temperature has been soaring at 38C plus, and it is worrying.

This morning I went to the doctor's after she declined to visit, having been yesterday when Lesley was looking better. I urged Val and my mum to rouse Lesley whilst I went to demand a visit. Her temperature has been up to 40C and we really don't understand what is happening . . . and that's when it all kicks off.

Whilst I'm talking with the doctor, my dad phones my mobile to say they have called for an ambulance. Her mum is concerned at not being able to wake her. Then, before I've finished, my dad rushes into the doctor's office to say the ambulance has arrived and Lesley is being taken down to casualty. I immediately leave and start to run down the road. As I approach, I can see the ambulance outside the house, and as I arrive Lesley is being lowered down the stairs by the medics and rushed off to A & E. Val accompanies her whilst I follow in the car. Lesley is unconscious. When I arrive at casualty she is laid out on a bed with lots of people round her as they discuss what to do. About thirty minutes and lots of needles and drips later, they call for an immediate brain scan to assess the situation. We are then led off into a side room to wait.

After about an hour we are called back in. The situation is serious. She has an empyema, which is a pocket of infection sitting on the outer part of the skull and putting pressure on her brain. It must be drained or she will die within forty-eight hours. By this time, Lesley's dad has arrived and we have a discussion with the surgeon. I explain the situation to him and ask whether we are putting her through too much, bearing in mind her terminal diagnosis. It feels like an impossible situation. Ultimately I will have to sign the consent for the operation and I have some doubts. Surgery of this severity is not without risk in previously healthy people – and Lesley has been far from healthy. In the end, we ask for some direct advice from the surgeon. He is without doubt. 'If this was my sister, then I would operate.' We discuss it between ourselves. All this has happened so quickly, without preparation or warning; she could be taken without having said goodbye. The power to give her that choice now lay in our hands . . . the operation would go ahead. I signed the necessary forms and Lesley was prepared and taken to theatre.

Eight hours is a long time to wait for someone to return from surgery and we had no idea what to expect, but when the registrar came to see us late that night in a small, dimly lit side room on the neurological ward at the QMC,[19] what she said was definitely not what we had expected. Lesley had come through the operation, was now in recovery and would be brought up to the ward as soon as she was stable. 'She has undergone a serious operation to remove a large amount of pus from her brain,' she told us, 'you can expect her to be in hospital for up to six weeks.' We looked at each other – shocked. Six weeks! I never realized that people can be in hospital to recover for so long.

The next day I arrived at 9.30 a.m. having been given special permission by the sister to come and see Lesley post op. The previous night we had seen her brought back to the ward with an 8 inch cut on the right side of her head. Apart from that, she was still dazed from the anaesthetic. 'Go home and get some rest,' the nurse said. 'You can come back and see her early in the morning.' We left and went home to bed, exhausted.

As I walked onto the ward I could hear the most terrible screaming, worse than I'd ever heard. I knew the person screaming was Lesley. The nurses were trying to give this terrified, weak and confused young woman a wash. They didn't know what they had let themselves in for. As she screamed and screamed, she kicked out and pushed them away, the bowl of water spilling all over the floor – it was chaos. I immediately went to her and she looked at me, struggled to communicate, and wailed. She was completely traumatized, not knowing where she was or what had happened. The last thing Lesley knew was lying in her own bed at home. Now here she was, confused, in pain, and unable to properly communicate, having undergone major surgery twelve hours before. She looked at me and muttered some desperate words. It was the worst hour of my life.

I left the ward soon after to make some phone calls. My first was to her mum, Val. 'Lesley is in a terrible state,' I said. During my time on the ward, I'd almost begged the sister to sedate Lesley, to at least give her some rest from her distress. She explained to me that they don't sedate neurological patients, since they need to measure progress by observation. They hoped to see steady improvement as each day passed by, and to administer antibiotics to bring the infection under control. This was going to be a long six weeks.

It's amazing how quickly you adjust to new surroundings. After a week or so, Ward D10 at the QMC became like a second home. Somehow, we'd managed to extend visiting hours to an extent that we were covering 10 a.m. in the morning to 11 p.m. in the evening. I'm not quite sure how we did it, but the routine soon developed whereby I would drop Val at the hospital for 10 a.m., then arrive myself for 2 p.m. and stay till 7 p.m., when Val would arrive with her husband, David. They would then cover the evening whilst I went home to put Charlotte to bed to try to maintain a routine for her. Meanwhile, back at the house, my own parents moved in and acted as major back-up, providing collection services for Charlotte from school, and doing washing, cooking and shopping. The whole process was executed with military precision.

As each week passed, Lesley would get a visit from the main consultant, Mr White. 'You've been very lucky,' he told her on one of his bedside visits. 'Over 40 per cent of people die from what you contracted.' Barry White was amongst the best neurosurgeons in the land, the staff told us; he always wore pale trousers, shirt and bow tie, which along with his greying hair and round glasses made him a distinct, if not slightly eccentric, character. But for all his comments, I'm not sure that Lesley felt lucky, and neither did I. If anything, it felt as if 'luck' might be running out. In going forward I hoped we could build on something more than 'luck', anyway. Yet somewhere deep inside I knew what he meant. From here on, each day was truly a gift.

You soon learn that hospitals are hierarchical institutions. There is a person for everything and every person has their place. It's not until you are on an extended stay that the barriers of professionalism come down, and the institution gives way to real humanity. The people behind the uniforms are human, just like the patient in the bed. They have homes to go to and children to look after or, in the case of one of the young nurses who looked after Lesley, friends to go out and party with! The patient too, over time, becomes more than a person to be cared for, but a human being with fears and worries; someone who has a life outside of those four walls which, for now at least, has come crashing down around them. Each one needs love, emotion and warmth. Care is not simply about giving the body food and medicine; it's also about communicating information with accuracy and sensitivity. Yet each day in these hospitals decisions are made, news is given and operations performed that change people's lives forever. Every day, people in positions of power and trust hold massive sway over the sick and vulnerable as they hang on every word and hope for the best possible outcome. If nowhere else in our sanitized western society, hospitals are still the places where people are brought face to face with their own mortality. And you don't have to be the patient in bed to know; simply being there is reminder enough that life can hang by a thread for any one of us.

After the first week we were well settled in to our routine, and the restaurant across the corridor became not only a place to eat food, but also a meeting point for friends that popped by to visit. Over the weeks of Lesley's stay, I met numerous people either there or in the WRVS café in the main reception. I became a regular, ordering my usual latte.

Back on the ward, the routine became something of a ritual that provided the framework for each day. The nurse came to take blood pressure and temperature, and to administer the medicines. The auxiliaries brought the food menu and turned up with breakfast, lunch and tea, and the various beds round the ward were visited by friends and family during visiting hours. From time to time, a ward doctor would come and take blood or check dosages of medication, and this routine continued day in, day out. Now and then, patients would press buzzers to get the attention of the nurses, and wait until they were able to attend – a trip to the toilet, assistance to get a drink, a concern that medicines were running late and so on.

As a regular visitor, spending at least six hours on the ward every day for over five weeks, you become a familiar face, and conversations about life outside the ward develop. Apart from those conversations, and chatting with patients and visitors from the other beds in the bay, my routine developed into checking Lesley over when I arrived, allowing her to sleep, and settling down to read the daily newspaper. Then, about 4 p.m., I'd make a trip down to the café for my latte, then back to the ward with a copy of the *Evening Post* which, after tea, Lesley would briefly look over. When tea arrived, I'd assist her in sitting up and preparing, making sure we had adequate tissues nearby, and then manoeuvring the bed tray so she could reach her food comfortably. I'd then sit and hope that the food she'd ordered the previous day resembled in some way what actually arrived on the plate. I'm sure hospital food has improved over the years, and they certainly seem to be trying hard, but it's never going be to five star! For the first couple of weeks, eating anything was a struggle, but slowly it improved and by the end of her stay she was back to eating food at each meal time.

In addition to eating is the question of mobility and, after such a massive operation, the lack of it. To stand up by the side of the bed was all Lesley could manage for quite some time, and over that period I genuinely wondered if things would ever improve. Meanwhile the doctors, nurses and other staff continued with their routines with the quiet assurance that things would, over time, get better. They'd seen it all before; this strange world into which we'd be plunged was everyday life for them – without the emotional attachment. But for us and the other five patients who made up the bay, it was really daunting and quite scary.

After the end of the second week, it was time for the staples to be removed from Lesley's head. There were seventeen of them holding together a wound of about five inches, and as each one was extracted the wound held together, afterwards revealing a neat, clean scar which became the only physically visible remnant from the operation. I winced as the doctor removed each one. Lesley didn't.

Lesley was in the end bed on the left-hand side of the bay, facing a large window overlooking the main entrance below with all its coming and goings. It proved to be a useful distraction, and many times I would stand and look out of the window at the people as they came and went throughout the day. Taxis would pull up and collect people, and ambulances would drop off day patients and then, later, take them home. Those fortunate to be visiting for work reasons were fewer in number and easily recognized by the suits they wore – like the woman in her mid thirties who pulled up one day in her metallic silver Audi TT and negotiated a parking space with the attendant; he kindly moved a cone for her to park, and then smiled as he watched her struggle to reverse into the space. Perhaps, like me, he was jealous of her car! The rest going through reception wore either a nurse's uniform or regular casual clothes; no one was getting dressed up for a day out.

When it was time for Lesley to go home I found myself quite emotional, as if we were leaving behind friends. We swapped numbers with a few, and changed email addresses with others. 'Let's keep in touch,' I said. And we did, for while, but it soon dropped off.

Arriving back home that day was really strange. It was now late November and as Lesley sat down on the settee, she said she felt as if she didn't belong there any more. She could see how life had gone on whilst she'd been away. The kitchen had become the domain of my mother, who cooked each day for everyone, the garden the domain of my father, who tended it and planted at his own discretion. The hallmarks of ownership were slowly slipping away, and as she cried and told me how she felt I understood it implicitly but felt unable to change it, at least for now.

It would be a few more weeks before we got back to any sense of normal home life, but eventually the day did arrive when both sets of parents left us. It was really strange at first, and I think we all knew that life would never be quite the same. The impact of the emergency operation was massive and regular follow-ups became part of our lives. We were always on the lookout for tell-tale signs of infection, changes which might call for a quick decision on our part. The steroids had been stopped as soon as the infection had been identified and would play no further role in either pain management or energy lifts. That would become the job of painkillers, and paracetamol often came to the rescue.

Christmas was now the next goal to reach, and earlier in the year we'd agreed with Lesley's side of the family to spend it together in a large cottage in the Derbyshire Dales. The decision had been made prior to Lesley's operation and became a helpful focus. We all had something to aim for, and when Lesley was really struggling, it became a useful source of encouragement: 'Let's help you get better so we can all go away together,' we'd tell her.

Lesley, along with her sister-in-law, had been the main people behind the idea of a change at Christmas. They wanted to break away from the usual routines and do something different, and sourced the place together on the Internet. And, whilst in hospital, the planning for it on her better days became a useful distraction. So, as December arrived, the final preparations were made, and on the twenty-third we packed up the car and set off.

We spent the best part of a week together, sitting around playing games, watching TV and challenging each other on Brain Training on the Nintendo. At other times, a few of us would go off for walks, or a drive out in the car, which made it possible for Lesley to come along. She was quiet a lot of the time and struggled, but we all made the effort to make the time away enjoyable. I guess in the back of all our minds we knew this would be her last Christmas and I remember holding back the tears on Christmas Day as that prospect loomed heavy on me. I'm not sure what the others thought – I never asked them – but for me it was a bittersweet time. When we arrived back home a week later, I could tell the trek had taken its toll on her. Early that evening Lesley was asleep on the settee, leaving Charlotte and I to play with her new toys.

And so, with Christmas over and the New Year upon us, we resumed what was our new routine: different parts of the week were spent on our own, then other times one set of parents would come and support, taking on practical jobs, allowing me to get out at night for a meeting here or a visit to the pub there. The weeks passed by in similar fashion with things on the outside establishing an ever-so-slowly deteriorating pattern, but inside the pressure and storms of life sometimes raged.

Chapter Five 2008

When Evening Shadows Fall

When evening shadows fall,
She hangs her cares away
Like empty garments on the wall
That hides her from the day;
And while old memories throng,
And vanished voices call,
She lifts her grateful heart in song
When evening shadows fall.
Her weary hands forget
The burdens of the day.
The weight of sorrow and regret
In music rolls away;
And from the day's dull tomb,
That holds her in its thrall,
Her soul springs up in lily bloom
When evening shadows fall.
O weary heart and hand,
Go bravely to the strife –
No victory is half so grand
As that which conquers life!
One day shall yet be thine –
The day that waits for all

Whose prayerful eyes are things divine
When evening shadows fall.
                    James Whitcomb Riley, 1849–1916[20]

Saturday 8 March 2008   1,113 days after diagnosis
It's 9.45 p.m. and Lesley has just gone off to bed without
saying anything to me. No 'goodnight' or 'I need to go
up to bed' or 'I hate your silence' . . . nothing. Just got up
off the settee after I asked if she wanted to come over for
a cuddle, and then off to bed. Ought I go up to her and
lie with her? Yet, to do that is just to be pushed off again;
I'm not sure I have the energy for that, and neither has
she.

I never thought life would come to this – Lesley and I
torn apart in this way. I listened in to her speaking with
her mum earlier. To hear her speak is to know how
awful I am in her sight nowadays. I can't believe that she
would ever speak about me in such dismal ways to her
parents; honestly, I am living with someone else – this is
not even close to the person I once knew.

Charlotte asked again today why her mummy is so
horrible to her sometimes. I desperately try to cover
those moments with humour, distraction and the occasional snippet of information about the fact that
Mummy sometimes has pains in her head. The discussion today came after Lesley shouted at her for not looking hard enough to find her vest. Life can be tough when
you're 7, eh?

We went to see Mr Ward at Sheffield this week. It was
Lesley's regular appointment with him. It's a very surreal experience speaking with him. He questions the value
of us going along. He has nothing to offer, which makes
him feel bad, especially since Lesley is so appreciative of
his time and, in his words, 'so young' – so young to
be facing what she is facing; he feels so powerless, as a

surgeon and consultant, to help. We came away with a further appointment in three months' time. He suggests we might better using our precious time shopping.

As we drive home, I ask Lesley how she feels about the appointment. Is it any help to her? 'Yes, it is,' she concludes. 'At least he understands the process of what is happening, and it allows me to ask him questions.' I think I understand. We all need to talk.

Tuesday 25 March 2008
Infection is back; I can tell, and smell it on her breath. Yesterday we had taken a trip to A & E with a spiking temperature of up to 40C. By the time we got there and an assessment had been made, it was back to normal and Lesley was feeling better, so they sent her home. You sort of know it's not going to last, and today we are faced with the same issues, so we call for the local GP. She takes a look at her, asks a few questions and says we can't take the risk, so she writes a referral for that afternoon. After a drink and bit of lunch I pop upstairs, and a short time later Lesley joins me. We embrace, and look at each other with a deep sense of foreboding; we've been this way before. This will be no short visit; we both know nothing is straightforward nowadays.

When we arrive we sit in a packed assessment ward full of people of all ages with cuts and bruises, and a whole manner of ailments. It's time to prepare for a long wait. It's been Bank Holiday weekend and this is the first day that GPs have been back to normal hours, so everyone and their uncle have been sent down for assessment. As we sit there, and I look at Lesley, I have a mad moment and ponder the possibility that her temperature is not actually an infection, but rather God's intervention to burn up the tumour in her head. It's a moment of madness maybe, but one of faith too.

We'd prayed on Sunday for Lesley, asking God to intervene with healing. She had stood in humility and obedience at the front of the church and we called together in prayer for God to act; it was Easter Sunday, after all – if that day was not about a miracle, then what was?

So now, here I am thinking about that possibility. Daring to believe that our simple, maybe foolish, but nevertheless faithful, prayers might have an effect. Apparently, they didn't – at least not in the way we'd hoped. I've discovered a lot of my prayers have been like that over the past few years – it does make you wonder.

After about two hours we finally get moved to one of the assessment bays and the process begins. First it's the paperwork, then the questions and finally the examination. The doctor is really helpful, friendly and competent, and despite his age (early forties) was still a junior, having taken a late career change from pharmacy. His wife had suffered breast cancer a few years back and recovered, and the experience had caused a life change for him – he wanted to give something back.

His initial examination, followed by blood tests, confirmed our original suspicion that an infection was present somewhere in her body. A hospital stay was now certain, so off to the ward we went. It was going to be a long few weeks.

Arriving on a new ward late at night is always disconcerting. You feel a real sense of disorientation compounded by worry and anxiety. Lesley is situated next to and opposite two old men, both of whom are crying out for help. It's late, dark, and Lesley is crying and upset. We stay around for some time, helping to get her settled. Tomorrow they will run further tests and decide what her next move will be.

Wednesday 26 March 2008

There's some debate going on between neurology and ENT as to which ward Lesley should be moved to, since her condition falls between the two. As the day unfolds it becomes clear that a decision will be made soon. Meanwhile, she will stay where she is on B5. Towards the end of the day she is concerned not to have received the results of the CAT scan, and requests the nurse to ask a doctor for them before I leave for the evening. After some time one of the duty doctors arrives, draws the curtains round the bed, and sits down to tells us sympathetically that it's not good news.

Since Lesley's condition is complex, any doctor reading her scans for the first time always paints a very bleak picture, and tonight is no exception. After a fifteen minute conversation, we are left with an open access policy for our visits to the ward, and the impression that Lesley's condition is deteriorating rapidly and might not improve. Once the doctor has left, she panics and immediately phones her mum and dad to come right away. They respond and leave immediately, no doubt wondering what situation they will find when they arrive.

About 11 p.m., with only the nightlights to see by, Dave brings Val onto the ward and round to Lesley's bed. We are both half asleep; I'm slouching in the bedside chair. In the rush, Val has fallen down some hospital steps and is in a wheelchair.

As we wake from our slumber, all I can hear is Val saying, 'I can't believe it. I just can't believe it.' None of us can believe it. How can an impossibly difficult situation get any worse? And yet it just has – and the seriousness of it all actually brings a smile to our faces. Here we are, sitting round the bed of my wife – and their daughter – who is struggling with terminal cancer, trying to absorb yet more news of the imminence of what she faces, and we're *laughing* at the new predicament we find ourselves in. How can life get this bad?

After an hour or so, Dave wheels Val off to A & E and I stay with Lesley on our newly given open access policy. At 3.30 a.m. I am woken by the sound of voices and the squeaking wheel of Val's chair. She is back from casualty, complete with her foot in plaster; she has fractured it in three places, rushing to be with her daughter. For sixty years she has been fracture-free, but tonight she has scored a hat-trick.

About 4.30 a.m. we finally leave the ward and head down to the car park. Val hobbles out of the chair and into their car, and they go back to Chesterfield. I walk round to the multi-storey, drop into my car and head off home. Tomorrow, I will be back for another day.

Thursday 27 March 2008
Today is the start of a new and somewhat familiar routine, one well rehearsed from last year since once again infection threatens Lesley's life, and a prolonged stay in hospital becomes inevitable. Weary at the thought, we all rally round as best we can but there are a few differences from before. The infection is not in the same place as the previous one, and scans reveal it is directly linked to the tumour site. There is no build-up on the brain and therefore no operation required. It is bad, though, and the only means they have to bring it under control is to administer IV antibiotics like before. It will be at least a two- or three-week course.

Meanwhile, back in Chesterfield, Val is getting worse. It is discovered that not only has she got a broken foot but she has also contracted food poisoning. She is laid up in bed with chronic sickness and unable to walk anywhere since the broken foot has now turned painful, and has swollen badly. Unlike before, she will not be available to help with any of the visiting; the bulk of that will be left to Dave and me. We're not allowed the same level of access, either: the emergency access granted on Ward B52 is removed and we are told to use visiting hours only, so I cover 2 p.m. to 6.30 p.m., then David arrives and stays to the end of visiting, which can be stretched a little, depending on the staff nurse.

It's not long before I slip back into my old visiting routine of reading papers, drinking coffee and eating my way through a packet of Revels. Lesley is asleep for the majority of the time I am there, knocked out by both the infection and the drugs they are using to treat it. One evening, just before tea, her consultant arrives. He pulls up a chair, sits down and asks how she is doing. He explains the serious nature of the infection, how the situation might deteriorate, and how limited they are in being able to respond to it. 'We will help you as much as we can, Lesley,' he tells her. 'It's really up to you how much you want to fight.' He discusses her scans and the results of her latest blood test, and once again highlights how limited they are in terms of what they can offer. 'I think infection is the way this tumour will get you in the end,' he says. It's a rather abrupt conclusion to our conversation, but then we did ask for his honesty.

The next few weeks come and go in what feels like an eternity. Coming and going, coming and going builds a routine that I find draining, which is odd when you consider that you aren't doing much other than sitting there and waiting, and then waiting some more. Lesley has had a few extra visitors over the weeks, but not many, preferring to be left alone, and not feeling up to 'putting on a face' to meet people.

After three weeks, the IV antibiotics are finished and she is discharged. She's weaker leaving the hospital than she was before she arrived, so they provide a wheelchair and a nurse comes with us to help her to the car. It's teatime, as we leave the hospital and start the slow drive back home. When we arrive we are welcomed by everyone, and Lesley lies down on the settee. Another chapter has closed and the next is about to open, but at this stage no one knows how it will be written.

Wednesday 23 April 2008
Tonight Lesley asked if we could all pray together. We gathered round the bed and I led a prayer, muttering words and stumbling over my sentences, since prayer has become a much more difficult and reflective process over the past year or so. Afterwards, my dad prayed and so did Lesley. She poured her heart out to God in love and sincerity – it was without bitterness or resentment, and full of love and passion – quite beautiful. She expressed the depth of her feeling to God, and how she feels about us, her 'lovely family'. Afterwards she spoke to my mum and told her how much she loved her and has been loved by her. These are special times, holy moments when somehow God breaks through the pain and we are touched by something pure and precious, rather like being washed in clean water.

Earlier, the district nurse arranged a new bed with an air mattress to help prevent pressure points turning into bedsores. Lesley spends a lot of time in bed now. Since being in hospital she has not been out of the house, and is struggling to make a simple walk from the bedroom to the bathroom. Each step is measured, every one an effort resulting in pain or discomfort of some form or other. The nurse has been really helpful and proactive; nothing has been too much trouble.

Monday 5 May 2008

Lesley is dressed and downstairs. Its lunchtime and we've made plans to take a little trip out. All of us are off to Attenborough Nature Reserve, where there is a café and area to sit and enjoy the views overlooking the lake. After we have parked, we get out the wheelchair and set off for the café. It's a busy Bank Holiday afternoon and it appears everyone has had the same idea. The place is packed with people enjoying some early summer sunshine. When we arrive at the café, it's full, and we steadily manoeuvre Lesley round in her wheelchair to a table situated at the far end facing a window that overlooks the lake. After about twenty minutes, we drink up and set off back to the car. We don't stay anywhere long these days; just time enough to sit down, drink coffee and then head back. But at least we have all been out together and ventured into the sunshine.

When we arrive back home, I offer to make some tea. Tonight it will be ostrich burgers – a new experience for everyone. I'm just finishing off, and taking them out of the grill to place on a new fresh cob with some salad, when her mum comes in. 'Lesley's mouth is bleeding. What do we need to do?' This is the second time it's occurred. The first was a week or so earlier, and we'd all been in a real panic, wondering what was happening. This time we were a little wiser, not less anxious, but at least knowing that it would, after a while, slow down and stop.

The bleed is coming from the top part of her mouth, where the tumour has invaded the soft palate and begun to erode some of the blood vessels in that area. This time, however, the bleed is looking a bit worse; it's taking longer to stop and there are some very large clots of what appear to be congealed lumps of flesh and blood. She coughs one up as I enter the room. I immediately heave and run to the bathroom, throwing my guts up.

What a coward! I calm down: I'm not great with blood, and the size and amount took me by surprise.

An hour later, and with a carrier bag half full of bloody tissues, all is calm. We settle down for the evening. The burgers end up in the bin. Well, I wasn't that hungry in any case.

Thursday 8 May 2008
Lesley had an ENT appointment today. We sat patiently in the waiting room, sipping water from a white plastic cup provided from the dispenser situated close to reception. About ten minutes later we took our place outside the consultation room, waiting our turn. When we were called through, Lesley sat down with the consultant and rehearsed something of her now familiar – if uncommon – medical history. Sitting opposite were two others, both ladies: one a doctor, the other a nurse. This was the Thursday multidisciplinary team. Every patient here today was either dealing with cancer, or coping with its after-effects.

It's not every day you meet a new oncologist, and not every day that one of them sits talking and explaining that, from what they can see from your latest scan, it is time to 'make your end of life plan'. 'Take each day as it comes and each week as it arrives' was her advice to Lesley. Her name was Doctor Christian, a slim lady in her early forties, with shoulder-length dark hair and a Scottish accent. Understandably, Lesley was blown away. No one had ever spoken to her with such clarity about her illness. She, like me, understood the terminal diagnosis that had been given a couple of years previously, but now a professional, someone who dealt with cancer every day, was looking at Lesley and, from what she had seen and noted from her scan, speaking to her about how the cancer had progressed and was picking up pace in its destructive path. The oncologist went on to explain how the cancer was demanding more of her energy so it could grow, which was one of the reasons for her tiredness. She could expect things to go downhill from here – and it may happen quickly. 'You need to be prepared, to make your plans and have things in place.' She was talking about weeks! 'If you are not any better in two weeks, then that will be a good gauge of how the cancer is progressing,' she said. 'If, on the other hand, in a month's time you are as well or better than you are now, then things may have stabilized slightly.'

As we left the room and walked towards the exit, Lesley was beside herself with worry. She didn't want to go back home; didn't want to stay away: confusion and fear reigned.

Sunday 11 May 2008
I'd planned to go for a drink later in the evening with friends Caz and Steve. The Admiral Rodney, our local pub, is what I had in mind.

But that afternoon, my plans change. Lesley is anxious about how much time I spend away from home. Rather than going out, I arrange for them to come over to the house, where we can spend some time chatting over a Coke and whisky in the summer house, and in that way Lesley can join us too. This change of plan is also for Charlotte's benefit; she is getting more agitated and upset whenever I leave the home. It's hard to tell the effect all this upheaval to what used to be our normal routine is having, but obviously it is beginning to tell in her behaviour. She is fretting deeply for her dad.

At 8.30 p.m. our friends arrive and we walk the length of the garden to the large summer house at the bottom. In usual circumstances it would be a perfect end to a lovely, hot summer's day, but these days are as far from

normal as you can get. Lesley joins us for the first part of
the evening, and she has something to say to her friends
by way of a goodbye.

We start with general chit-chat about this, that and
nothing. After ten minutes, Lesley takes over the conversation. 'I'm pleased you have been able to come
tonight because I want to talk to you.' She then goes on
to explain something of the conversation she had in the
week about the progression of her cancer and the effect
this is having on her. 'My time is coming to an end. They
have clearly told me that this week. God's time for my
life on earth will soon be over. Take all that life has to
offer and make the most of everything. I want you to go
on and live, live, live,' she tells them with utter sincerity.
'Love each other and serve God. I will be there cheering
you on and waiting to meet you in heaven. And please,
please, look after this man for me. Help him and support
him; he's going to really need that in the future.'

All of us in the room are wrecked by her words. She
stands up, hugs them deeply and then says she wants to
leave and go back to the house. 'I can't do those things
we used to do any longer,' she tells Caz, one of her closest and dearest friends. 'I just don't have the energy any
more, and my mind won't allow me to think clearly.'

I walk her slowly back to the house, feeling her frailty
as I put my arm round her waist to support her. She
knows her time is short. Tonight was a further step in
her preparations for the end. Once again, through tears
and pain I had stood on holy ground.

Tomorrow we will meet the hospice doctor from the
specialist palliative care team.

Monday 12 May 2008   1,179 days after diagnosis
Tonight Charlotte asked what I'd dreaded for so long: Will
her mummy die? How do you answer such a question

from a 7-year-old; how can you explain that her mummy will die, and possibly quite soon?

A couple of weeks earlier I had explained to her that Mummy had a disease called cancer.

'Cancer, cancer,' she said. 'You might as we tell me she has . . . well I don't know what to say, but "cancer" doesn't mean anything to me.' Trying not to forget I'm speaking to a young girl, I come up with an idea.

'Why don't I draw you a picture to try to explain what cancer is?' I replied.

'That's a good idea, Daddy,' she said. 'Go and get some paper.'

And so I popped to the office and came back with a pen and notepad. We proceeded to draw a picture of a body.

'All our bodies are made up of cells,' I told her. 'Now, there are lots and lots and lots of these cells in our body, and most of the time they all live together happily like really good friends, and that makes our body healthy. But sometimes one of these cells will decide it doesn't want to be friends any more and so tries to make its own cells. And these cells fight the good cells and that is called a cancer.'

By now we've had the cancer conversation on a few occasions. Each time I get the notepad, draw a picture of the body, make little circles to represent cells, and explain how one of these cells has turned bad and started to make bad friends. We'd progressed to the extent where we started writing on the paper the different effects that the cancer was having on Mummy's body. Loss of an eye, no taste, no smell, loss of hearing, lack of jaw movement, loss of teeth, the list went on.

Finally, we arrived at the stage where Charlotte wanted to know what happens – she picked up the pen to illustrate – if the cancer started to grow here and here and here . . . aggressively drawing strong black lines all over the body we'd already drawn. I knew she was trying to make a point; in her mind she knew more than she was saying. I explained, 'If the cancer keeps growing, Charlotte, then the person eventually dies.' And now, this evening, we've got to the stage of explanation where death was going to relate specifically to her mummy, and she asks me directly, 'Daddy, is Mummy going to die?'

'Yes, Charlotte, Mummy is going to die,' I reply.

She immediately bursts into tears.

It's taken some time to get to this place. To have the confidence that speaking so honestly is the right thing to do. I'd pondered this occasion many times in my mind over the past few years, agonizing over how I would broach the issue and what I might say. But here we are, at 8 p.m. on a sunny summer's evening in May, lying together on her bed surrounded by pink walls and Disney pictures, and the issue I'd so feared is now in the open. I have finally told my only daughter that her mummy will die from cancer. As a father, it is difficult to imagine anything more difficult than this, apart from perhaps the moment of death itself.

After a few minutes, she stops crying and jumps up. She's off to find her mum.

'I've got something to tell you,' I say to Lesley as we arrive downstairs. 'Charlotte just asked me a very important question.'

Charlotte listens intently to my words.

'She asked if you were going to die,' I say, looking at Lesley with a reassuring glance to try to affirm tonight was the right time. 'She asked if Mummy was going to die and I had to answer her honestly and say, "Yes, you are".'

Her mum confirms what I have said. She has now heard from both of us. Charlotte starts to cry again.

The three of us head upstairs to her bedroom, leaving both grandparents in the lounge. We go into her room and sit together on the bed. Lesley then starts to reassure Charlotte that her dying is nothing to do with her. That she really, really does not want to die, and that the doctors have done everything possible to try to stop the cancer, but it didn't work.

'I don't want you to die, Mummy, I don't want you to die,' Charlotte cries.

'I know. I know you don't, Charlotte,' I reply. 'None of us wants Mummy to die, and it is making us all very, very sad.'

Sometime later, Lesley's mum comes into the room and the questions start again. 'Did you know Mummy was going to die, Nana?'

'Yes, Charlotte.'

'When did you know?'

'Not too long ago.'

'Why didn't you tell me before?'

It's the start of a barrage of questions which you neither anticipate nor prepare for. During the course of the next hour, everyone in the house is called to the bedroom and questioned by this young and inquisitive mind. It's as if a safety valve has been triggered, and all the questions, most of them repeated to each person, pour out like steam from a pressure stove. At the bottom of it appears to lay one main issue. Why has she not been told before? How could it be that other people knew that her mummy was going to die, before she did? Somehow, in the mind of a 7-year-old this could not be right.

Slowly, I start to reassure her that she has been told at the right time, and before other people. I go on to explain that I needed to be sure from the doctors that Mummy would die, before I could tell her. She's not completely happy with that response, but she accepts it

– at least for now – and, after a lot more talking, finally drifts off to sleep. Tomorrow would be another day.

Tuesday 13 May 2008
'I don't want to go to school today, Daddy.'
'Why not, darling?'
'Because Mummy might die while I'm at school.'
'Don't worry, Mummy won't die today,' I reassure her.

After breakfast, we set off walking to school. As we walk up the road, we begin to talk about the night before. The comments keep coming.

'When I get to school, I'm going to tell the teachers about Mummy going to die.'
'Are you, darling? Is that what you would like to do?'
'Yes, but only the teachers. I don't want to tell the children, they won't want to play with me any more.'

The conversation then turns to the main issue of last night: why she wasn't told sooner. She goes on to say, 'I already knew that Mummy was going to die.'

'You did?' I respond, in a shocked tone of voice. 'You mean, all this time you have known that Mummy was going to die and you never told me? If you knew, Charlotte, then why didn't you tell me before?'

'Because I didn't want to make you sad,' she replied.

'And that's why I didn't tell you sooner, Charlotte, because I didn't want you to be sad, either. But it's alright now, isn't it, because we can both be sad together and that's OK.'

We continue our walk to school, chatting about this somewhat surreal world. As we approach the school, I ask Charlotte if she would like me to speak to the teachers first. Yes, she would. And that is what I do.

Later that day, I call the school to arrange an appointment to see the head teacher. I arrive at 3 p.m. and am greeted by the receptionist, offered a cup of tea and led in to see Mrs Bradbury. We've met before on several occasions, all of which have been quite difficult and tinged with sadness, as I have endeavoured to keep the school informed of the journey we are on.

Mrs Bradbury, a competent, kind and capable lady, sits down next to me as we begin to talk. We all carry our own pain through life, and I know from previous conversations that her family has not escaped the challenges of cancer. Immediately there is empathy and warmth along with an identification of what we are facing. The connection and support reminds me we are not alone. Graciously, she allowed me to speak, bringing her up to speed with the present situation. I explain that last night Charlotte had asked whether her mum was going to die. I told her that I confirmed that that was the case, and that now she was fully informed of the situation. Her suspicions had been confirmed by me, so it was now OK for everybody to speak openly about the situation. In such terrible circumstances I hoped that at least the burden of secrecy had been lifted.

After about twenty minutes I leave, with plans in place for a further meeting where Lesley and I will meet both Mrs Bradbury and the head teacher from the new school which Charlotte will join in September. We are both keen that everything possible will be in place to support Charlotte during her time of loss. Lesley is especially eager to ensure that everything possible is in place.

Saturday 16 May 2008
It's been a thoroughly exhausting week. As I think back over a series of meetings and conversations, I fail to recall the amount of tears shed and words spoken. These are the ones I can remember:

Sunday
Meeting with our friends Caz and Steve – it ends in tears.

Monday
A two-hour meeting with Nicola and Dr Bisharat El-Khoury, the Macmillan nurse and specialist palliative care doctor from Hayward House.

A telephone conversation with Audrey Boot, a friend, talking about care for Charlotte and how Lesley is feeling.

A meeting with neurological consultant from QMC.

Time spent together in the summer house, where Lesley gives Charlotte a special gift she had purchased over a year earlier that would help her remember her mum's love for her.

A long conversation that led to Charlotte asking if her mum would die, followed by a further few hours of tears and conversations with everyone in the house.

Tuesday
Meeting with Mrs Bradbury – it ends in tears.

Further conversations with Charlotte.

Meeting with our friend Helen Fearn, discussing ongoing support for Charlotte after her mum dies.

Leadership meeting where Lesley came and told the group about what the consultant had told her – it ends in tears.

Wednesday
Intense and deep conversation between Lesley and I, both speaking of our love, with Lesley vouching her deep love and how much she feels I have helped and supported her over the years. We both cry.

Thursday
Phone conversation with John Pettifor – he cries.

Phone conversation with Tracy Fantom – she cries.

Friday
Phone conversation with Andrew Belfield – he cries.
  Visit from John and Pauline Pettifor – we all cry.
Saturday
Visit from Lesley's friend Shirley Abbott, an old school-friend of Lesley's and bridesmaid at our wedding – she cries.
  It's been a hard week.

Monday 19 May 2008
Lesley's temperature spiked at 38.2C yesterday, but this morning was back to a more respectable 37.4. We all breathed a sigh of relief. Another day without the need to call out the GP has passed.

A further card and letter arrived today. The card came from the family of a friend at Charlotte's school. It was thoughtful and simple – the type of card you appreciate and might think of sending yourself to someone in our situation.

It's amazing how much contact you get when you become a labelled family like ours. So many people want to help, and some people are able to express that better than others. It's also true that you are able to receive help from some people easier than from others – or at least, I can. The thing I find most difficult is help that's offered from people who have had little or nothing to do with you up until this crisis moment in life. Like an old contact from a decade or so earlier who sends a note with Scriptures to read at certain points of the day, to be taken like medicine. Or the person who feels they might be able to come and offer something by way of prayer if allowed a home visit. It's really difficult to handle these situations when you are vulnerable. Over the past few weeks I have been offered a book on prayer that guarantees answers if offered in a particular way; a contact

The baby years were some of Lesley's happiest as she doted over her new daughter.

Charlotte was a joyful addition to our home and a real delight to both her mummy and daddy.

I still remember taking this picture, and dreading deep inside what lay ahead of us as a family.

**Lesley and Charlotte attending a friend's wedding.
The first time Charlotte had been a bridesmaid and a
very happy occasion for us all.**

A fun day at the farm and one both Charlotte and I still fondly remember.

A brief respite (and massage) in Goa before heading off to Central India to visit an Orphanage.

The new arrival resting safely in the arms of her mummy.

Our last holiday together in Paris before Charlotte was born.

Taken in Gran Canaria, one of my favourites.

Lesley accompanying me on one of numerous humanitarian visits to Minsk, Belarus.

Two posers together, what more can I say!

Our Wedding Day –
Saturday, 27th October, 1990.

Sheffield Teaching Hospitals NHS
NHS Foundation Trust

Weston Park Hospital
Whitham Road Sheffield S10 2SJ

Tel: 0114 226 5000 Fax: 0114 226 5555

Please Reply to Dr O P Purohit
Consultant Clinical Oncologist

Tel (Direct Line): 0114 226506·
Fax: 0114 2265512

OPP/SJC/87/0504
NHS: 416 903 1261

27 August 2008

Mr S Hackney
96 Russell Drive
NOTTINGHAM
NG8 2BE

Dear Mr Hackney

I was very sorry to hear that Mrs Hackney recently passed away. Please accept my sincere condolences on your loss.

Mrs Hackney bore her illness with great strength and fortitude and I am sorry that we were unable to help her further.

If you or any members of your family wish to discuss any aspects of the illness or treatment with me, please feel free to contact my secretary on 0114 2265061 to arrange a mutually convenient date.

Kind regards

Yours sincerely

Dr O P Purohit

Cc
Mr S E Ward
Consultant Oral & Maxillofacial Surgeon
Charles Clifford Dental Hospital

A letter from Lesley's consultant.

This is now reall hay cney

First Mummy started to have canrer. And that made her have a Poorly eye, a Poorly Jaw, Speaking Problems, eating Problems, very thin,

Made her Poorly in bed had to go to the QMC then she came home. and all the nurse's and Doctors visited her they could'nt make her better so she had to go to haywood house and we stayed with her and she had no food or drink boo hoo. She couln't get better. So she died and Went to live with Jesus in heaven Lot wich is very Speacoial

Charlotte's letter: One of the saddest and most moving letters I have ever had to read.

for an alternative medical centre in South America, along with advice on the diet Lesley should now be taking; links to a revival in the States that claims healings are happening as people watch over the Internet . . . It's as if, all of a sudden, people I've not heard from in years are texting, calling or emailing. It's easy to understand why people who go through really difficult times want to cut themselves off. Simply handling the approaches of others can be exhausting. Each offer of help brings the need for a response, each response calls for a judgement, each judgement creates a reaction. It's really tiring, this illness stuff.

Of course, I have to remember that most, if not all, of these offers are prompted by human compassion and love. I'm sure the motivation of each person is to help. Paradoxically, most of the friends that are really close to me don't offer much help, advice or books to read. They simply listen to our story, what's new this month or week, and then cry. Afterwards, they might offer to take me for a coffee or a beer. That helps. As I said to a group of minister friends, mixing with me is complex. Don't ask how we are, and I think you don't care; ask how we are, and I think you are coming on too strong! As I say, 'Damned if you do; damned if you don't. You decide!'

Tuesday 20 May 2008
I woke this morning trying to work out how I get to the place of feeling resentment towards someone who writes a note, or sends a suggestion, with best intentions. It seems fair to assume their intentions to be good. And after some serious consideration I have concluded it has to do with proximity to the journey we are on; it's so much easier to take a prayer, suggestion or comment from those who have travelled the cancer journey with us, rather than from someone who has now heard the

gravity of our present position and gets in touch offering
a prayer or prescription that could lead to Lesley's deliverance from her illness. The difficulty is that they don't
write out of the pain; simply from the presumption that
to engage at this stage and attempt to say something positive is the right thing to do, not realizing that, sometimes, the right thing is to do nothing and simply quietly
pray or remember us. I think this is where the resentment
is based. I must simply learn to let it go.

I spoke with Val just before bed. I'd not been in too
long, having spent a few hours at the pub with one of
those friends who have travelled with us long enough to
know that letting me guide the conversation through the
evening is the best support he could possibly offer.

'It's such a roller coaster we are on,' she said. It's so
true. Lesley's approach to things can swing so dramatically in the course of a few hours that you are left not
knowing where you stand. At lunchtime, we were
together in the bedroom encouraging her to pull round
having listened to conversations about how time is running out and how she has left so many things undone.
She tells us how much worse she feels today than yesterday. It leads to the place where she writes a card to be
passed onto Charlotte after she has died, and we discuss how we might pass certain items of her jewellery
over at different points in her life. Both Val and I are left
emotionally drained by the episode. Later, Lesley is up
and dressed, feeling much better and, having watched
Charlotte take her first bike ride without stabilizers,
tells her mum how much better she feels. 'I feel like I
might be here for months yet, maybe even a year or
two.'

Whilst I'm out for the evening she suffers a strange
incidence of pins and needles running from her finger
up her arm and into the good side of her face. She is left

distressed by the experience; the roller coaster has just slid down into a dip, and rolls on.

Wednesday 21 May 2008
I've been acting selfishly of late by putting my own needs before other people's. I'd deliberately withdrawn to find solace and rest within myself whilst spending time thinking about the future, and it's not long before Lesley notices. She needs my presence, my contact, my touch and emotions now more than ever. That's the irony of illness; one party needs support at a time when the other feels least able to give it, and it creates a tension. Tonight, we tried to work through that tension.

At Lesley's prompting we spent some time together upstairs, chatting. Our chats nowadays can be, understandably, quite intense; not argumentative, just heavy. There is little lightness, no fun and very little laughter. We both recognized this and agreed to try to bring some of that laughter back. As we spoke, it reminded me of why I love her so much; she is such an able-minded and capable person. She has also been loved and supported by me during our marriage and knows when that is missing, and it's missing now. I'm not sure how much of that I can bring back, how much I can turn round, since I'm not sure of the degree to which I might have subconsciously withdrawn from the relationship as a self-protection mechanism. But one thing I do know: she deserves better.

As we left the bedroom having talked and listened, we smiled gently at each other. We might have been tested, but our love is still intact. As she walks downstairs and glances back at me with a look of gentle innocence, I realize again the love we had and how it has been both tested and taken by disease. Even now, Lesley knows clearly her own mind and its limitations; she knows what she is putting on me and asking of me. Her request is not unreasonable; she wants to know and feel the love upon which our whole relationship has been built. Surely that can't be too much for a wonderful woman struggling so bravely with terminal cancer to ask. The question is whether a man who dearly loves his wife, and has supported her every step of the way over four years and more, has the emotional strength to give it. I'm left wondering how on earth other people cope and keep going when faced by something of this enormity. I honestly can't imagine where we would be had we not had the foundation of a solid marriage to draw upon during these impossibly difficult times. There must be a lesson for everyone there somewhere.

Friday 23 May 2008
Andrew Belfield came to visit today, so I went into town for a walk around the city and stopped off for lunch at Strada, the Italian restaurant. Andrew has changed so much since his time in Nottingham, and conversations with him these days revolve, amongst other things, round our evolving theology. We're both so much more progressive in our thinking than we were ten years ago. It all seemed much simpler back then, and our belief system much more rigid. I explained some of my changing thinking in respect to expectation in the light of what appears to be less divine intervention. The premise of my argument goes along the lines of: 'Should God expect so much from us, if he is less willing or able to act significantly in our lives?' My thinking for such a harsh question is simple: if God makes such great demands of us, then surely commensurate to demand ought to be intervention – there needs to be proportional representation on both sides.

A couple of hours later we arrived back at home, and Andrew, Lesley and I spent half an hour together before he left, having promised to support Charlotte and I in the future. We all shed some tears and, as he left, Lesley said, 'I wonder if I will see him again?' I replied that I thought she would. She has made improvement of late which leads me to think that time has been extended for her.

Sunday 25 May 2008
Last night, Lesley texted several friends, asking them to pray she would make church the following morning. She had been desperate to attend all week, having missed the previous Sunday. She'd explained to me how important this was and how much her life had been moulded round this community of people and what that meant. It is true that, for the past twelve years, life revolved round the church – and more so since she had left her job in education to spend time with Charlotte. Now she wanted to be there to draw strength from the service and from her friends. So, before we went to sleep, we prayed and asked for God's strength, and I promised to do what I could the following morning to make it possible for her to attend, but ultimately that decision lay within her grasp and the constraints of her body.

At about 10.50 a.m. Lesley walked into church with her mum and dad and sat down on the back row. No one will ever understand the effort needed to make those steps possible, so when I stood up to speak I started to talk about her courage.

The church was low in numbers that morning and I'd spent a good proportion of the worship time questioning my own ability as a pastor. The church never seemed to grow past about fifty or sixty people and today about thirty were in attendance. A few weeks previously, someone had told me of their decision to leave, which is hard

not to take personally. Today, two from my small leadership group were not there. I suspect, without telling me
for fear of embarrassment, they had gone to one of the
larger churches in the city. Not that they shouldn't do
that of course, but it doesn't make things any easier
when you are already low and vulnerable, and it would
be courteous to be told.

As I continued to speak I found myself unsure of my
footing, not knowing what to say and what to leave out.
I spoke of my inadequacy and her bravery. I concluded
that the least we should do in support of her in light of
the effort she had made, was to pray. Even now, after all
these years, prayer seems the most appropriate response
to a situation that lies outside of human effort to resolve.
Even if prayer doesn't bring healing, I know that it can
bring comfort, and maybe that is healing, but in a different guise.

After five or ten minutes, our prayers were over.
Several people had spoken kind words, and I composed
myself and continued with the remainder of the morning.

After church, we left and headed home. It was Bank
Holiday and the Monaco Grand Prix was due to start at
1 p.m. Lesley had always dreamt of a trip to Monte
Carlo, but we've never quite made it. It was raining in
Monaco for the start of the race, and Lewis Hamilton
won.

Wednesday 28 May 2008
We went to see our friends David and Dorothy
Shearman tonight. We arrived at their house just after 6
p.m. and drove up the long drive, parked the car and
walked to the door, to be greeted by David, a long-
standing minister who has built a large church in the
centre of Nottingham. Both of them are in their mid

sixties, have seen life and don't suffer fools gladly. We step inside and take a seat in the lounge. They are compassionate, composed and considerate. They don't try to impress us with words, but simply offer us a drink, and we chat.

David was one of the first people I spoke to about the threat of Lesley's illness several years ago, and long before we got to the place of a definitive diagnosis. They've both been supportive over the years and, although we've not seen them too often of late, you feel a genuine sense of connection in their company. As the evening unfolds we chat about the things we have recently encountered, what the situation is at home, how we are coming to terms with the latest prognosis, and how we have attempted to take Charlotte on the journey of her mum's illness, dealing honestly and openly with her questions. It's an important time, a chance for Lesley to draw some reassurance that they will help support Charlotte and I when she has gone. They make their promises, we finish our drinks and, after an hour or so, prepare to leave. As we approach the front door, David takes Lesley's arm and leads her to the car; I stand slightly back and watch as he gracefully leads her and they gently chat. When we get to the car door, he opens it for her, sees her inside and looks at me. We both know we shouldn't be in this position, he sees the tear in the corner of my eye, and I notice the one in his. It's been my only show of emotion all night. I start the car and we head back home.

They'd both been impressed by the fact that Lesley had been well enough to go to their home, and this is the amazing thing about her. She has such determination, has so much to live for, and holds on with every ounce of energy she can muster. Part of the conversation had noted her bravery. Yet Lesley doesn't see herself as brave, and simply wants to be remembered as a loving wife and devoted mother. I doubt whether people will let her get away with simply that – to many she will be remembered as a woman who suffered with dignity, who took her illness and dealt with it with both faith and courage. That will certainly be David and Dorothy's remembrance.

Thursday 29 May 2008
The connection of life and illness has defined our home with a new sense of normality and today is no exception. The house is full of people, with both sets of parents filling all the bedrooms and me sleeping on the put-up bed in the lounge. Lesley's dad is up and off to work by 7.30 a.m., my parents are also up making an early morning drink, and I finally crawl out of bed about 8.15 a.m. wishing I could sleep for longer. I prepare Lesley's medication and then head off for a shower and prepare to take a morning jog.

When I get back home, I change and spend a couple of hours working before 1 p.m. when Nicola the Macmillan nurse is scheduled to visit. Today she is bringing a colleague, a social worker called Tina who specializes in family support. When they arrive, we chat in the lounge and outline to her how we are managing Charlotte's knowledge of her mum's illness. She reassures us that, from what we have said, we are taking all the right steps. At least that's a comfort. After an hour or so they leave and we prepare for a trip to town, but not before I get a call to request me to take a funeral service for an old man who has died.

After a short visit in town, we decide to eat out, and pay a trip to a local Italian restaurant. Afterwards, we dash back to the car park trying to dodge the rain, and Val hobbles along on her crutches with Charlotte trying to help. It's been an enjoyable few hours and everyone has stayed well.

Tonight, before we go to bed, Lesley reminds me that it's twenty-one years today that I first asked her out. It always amazes me how women can remember these things. We had a good smile about it. It's good sometimes just to treasure those moments and take them for what they are; to let the illness fall to one side, and enjoy the love that a committed relationship over all those years has to offer. I'd asked her out two decades ago whilst walking across Do It All car park on our way to buy some charcoal for a barbeque we were attending. I guess I never did quite hit the right tone in romance, but nevertheless she said yes and we shared our first kiss a few days later on a warm summer's evening in Linacre Woods, a local beauty spot. We'd driven there in my Mark One Ford Escort, which I'd bought from a friend for £100 and had to jump start each morning by rolling down the hill where I lived.

As we stand embracing each other on the landing before bed, Lesley is anxious. Tomorrow her mum needs to leave for a hospital appointment for her broken foot in Chesterfield, then plans to stay over and come back on Monday. She then reminds me again of her love for me, and reassures me about the wonderful life we have shared together. I agree. It has been wonderful. These last couple of years has tested us both to the point of breaking, but no one can take away the powerful memories of a love deeply shared between a man and woman. I assure her that she has had a really good day and she will be fine as we sleep overnight. We then part, me to the put-up bed in the lounge, whilst she goes off to sleep on the air mattress bed with her mum and dad next to her in our own double bed.

About 1 a.m. I'm still awake, sitting on the settee downstairs. By now, Charlotte, who's had a restless night, has come down to me, and I've tucked her into the bed opposite whilst I continue with some reading. I can hear noise upstairs and not long afterwards David arrives to say that Lesley can't sleep and she wants me. I immediately go to see her. She is having a convulsion with numbness in her arms, slurred speech and drifting in and out of alertness. Between us we check the obvious things. Is she choking? No. Is her breathing normal? Yes. Can she squeeze my hand with both arms? Yes. We refrain from panic, since it never helps, and Val continues to gently stroke her arm and reassure her. We pray. Then we wait, discussing our next move. Should we call the doctor, dial 999, or do nothing? After fifteen minutes, I call the doctor. Her seizure is going on longer and seems to be deeper than usual. We're all getting more anxious and, after twenty-five minutes with little improvement, we decide to call for an ambulance.

Five minutes later the medics arrive, and by now it's almost two in the morning and the blue lights of their vehicle illuminate the road. We lead them upstairs and they begin a process of checking Lesley over. After about an hour and a thorough check we decide it's best for her to stay at home and rest. The trauma of going to the QMC is outweighed by any gains she might receive. With the seriousness of her condition once again underlined but the immediate panic removed, we all settle down to sleep. By now the whole house has been woken and Charlotte is terribly restless. I agree to sleep with her to reassure her and provide some comfort. By 5.30 a.m. we are both still awake on what has already been a long night.

Saturday 31 May 2008
I'm feeling really flat today. It's 10 a.m., Lesley and Val are resting in bed and Charlotte has gone to join them.

My parents have gone off to tackle a job, and David left for work about 8 a.m. I'm thinking about the service at church tomorrow. We don't have anyone to lead worship since Dan is away for the weekend and our only keyboard player has left the church for greener pastures. I'd asked for help from one of the larger churches and they are trying to find someone to provide cover, so that will determine to a greater extent how things go.

So I decide to come back and think about options later. It's a glorious day outside and I reckon getting in the sunshine is a good antidote to my feelings.

Before I go out I decide to read from the Psalms. Today it's Psalm 3.

'O LORD, how many are my foes! How many rise up against me! Many are saying of me, "God will not deliver him." But you are a shield around me, O LORD; you bestow glory on me and lift up my head. To the LORD I cry aloud, and he answers me from his holy hill. I lie down and sleep; I wake again, because the LORD sustains me. I will not fear the tens of thousands drawn up against me on every side. Arise, O LORD! Deliver me, O my God! Strike all my enemies on the jaw; break the teeth of the wicked. From the LORD comes deliverance. May your blessing be on your people.'

It was an encouraging read.

Sunday 1 June 2008

Lesley made church again today. It's really important for her and makes a difference to how she feels.

Considering we were without any music for worship, the service seemed to go quite well. We had a break halfway through for coffee and doughnuts – it always seems to work!

This afternoon, Michael, Lesley's brother, came along with Karen, his wife. We had a nice time together and

Charlotte spent time playing with Karen in the garden. As they left, Lesley gave her brother a big hug and held his hand tightly. After they left, Lesley and I took a drive out in the car. It was an opportunity to get out of the house for her.

Monday 2 June 2008
Tonight Lesley and I went down to the church building to pray. About 9.30 p.m. she said she wasn't feeling at all well and wondered if we could go. When we arrived, we sat in the main room and prayed, and she poured out her heart to God for herself and me. She knelt down and prayed for my future, that it would be blessed, protected and prospered. She asked God that I might be the man he wants me to be, and live for him. It was the second time today we'd been in the position of talking about things related to life, death, funerals and the future. It's really exhausting for both of us. Earlier, Lesley told me how she felt that life was leaving her, and death was closer than she'd ever known. I just sat there, not knowing what to say. I mean, what do you say? When we got up to leave we held each other, kissed and prayed. The only comfort is Lesley's assurance that a place awaits her in heaven, and she has no doubt about that matter. But as for dying now, in this situation, and leaving us behind, I find she has little peace and no comfort, just a simple resignation to an impending inevitability.

Later, just after tea, as she prepares to wash her mouth in acerbic acid to help prevent bleeding, I take a look inside to see how things are. It's a terrible sight. Shining a small torch towards the back of her mouth reveals how the tumour has invaded the soft palate and extended the full length of the roof of her mouth on the right side. Further to that, the hole that was situated at the back has grown bigger. Last week I could see the small hole at the back right of her soft palate and it was about 5 mm. in diameter. Tonight it was easily 15 mm. It left me quite startled, since I'd not expected to see such a big change in a week. I tell Val about it, but not Lesley, since there seems little point in worrying her further. We both wonder what it all means. I decide that tomorrow I will email Lesley's old consultant Jeremy McMahon and ask him for an opinion, and if I can talk with him. Of course, he's not under any obligation to respond, so I will wait to see what happens.

Tuesday 3 June 2008
When I get back from taking Charlotte to school I sit down and write to Jeremy in Glasgow.

Hi Jeremy,
I trust you and the family are well and that your work in Scotland is progressing.

It seems quite some time now since we first met in your consultation room at Charles Clifford and Lesley's cancer has progressed significantly over the past six months or so. I think the last time I called she was having an emergency operation for an empyema from which she made a recovery but spent five weeks in hospital. The success of the treatment meant we were able to get away for a short break with the extended family over Christmas which we all enjoyed, albeit Lesley was limited in what she could do. In March she had a further infection that put her in hospital for another two weeks this time with an infection directly connected to the tumour site. The extension is now significant in that frontal part of her brain as well as right ear, sinus space and, as I look, the upper roof of her mouth. She has terrible black colouring on her tongue unlike anything I have seen and very limited jaw movement which leads to speech slurring and difficulty eating. Emotionally she is completely exhausted and understandably extremely fragile.

A few weeks ago I explained to Charlotte that her mummy was not going to get better and would die from her disease. Truly, those are the conversations you dread as a parent. I'd taken her on some quite considerable journey, allowing her to ask whatever questions she wished, answering them to the extent she asked, and then gradually raising the issue of naming the disease, drawing pictures of a body, then talking about how good cells which sometimes fall out with the others make their own friends which in turn forms a cancer – it seemed to help. I understand now that the management of the process is as important as anything else on this journey.

A few weeks back she had a couple of bad bleeds from her mouth which was really frightening at the time, and as a result we met up with the ENT team in Nottingham. We met a new oncologist who, having met us only that day, spoke kindly to Lesley about needing to make her end of life plans: 'Take each day as it comes and each week as it arrives, and if the weeks adds up to months then that is a bonus.' As hard as it was to hear (not that we are naïve to the ultimate outcome), I think it helped in allowing Lesley to do some of the things she has desperately put off in her courageous desire for life. As you will know, and of which we are now aware, a catastrophic bleed is a possibility of a life-ending scenario for her. We also have Macmillan Services and specialist palliative care team involved.

Over the past week I have noticed a small hole on the right side of her soft palate has grown from about 5 mm to 15 mm which is a very strange thing to see in someone's mouth. For a layman, what does that indicate – what lies beyond the hole!? To be honest, I wondered if we could perhaps have another call and chat about a few things. I understand if you'd prefer not to, since you have not seen Lesley in a few years, but her appointment at Charles Clifford has been deferred another month and a chat would be helpful from my perspective. I'd be happy to call you if you suggest a good time to ring.

    With best regards
    Stephen Hackney

I took Lesley to the charity shop today. We stayed about twenty minutes and afterwards she was ready to go home. The fact that she makes it anywhere at all is testament to how she keeps trying to press on. When we arrive back she is not feeling well and sits down with her mum to rest. Later, I collect Charlotte from school and take her to get a cake for my dad's birthday. Tomorrow he will be 70. We're back for tea at 5 p.m. and afterwards Lesley and I pop off for an hour to see our friends Steve and Caroline. Lesley is still terribly low when we arrive at the house and has a bad coughing fit, which doesn't help. She sits whilst I chat and listen to their holiday plans. They are off on Thursday to Greece for the week with some friends from Charis. It all seems a million miles away from our situation – a plane flight, a hotel, hot weather, late nights, relaxation; it just doesn't fit our radar.

    Terminal illness is not just hard on the person affected; it's hard on family and friends too. Steve and Caroline are amongst our best friends, and I can't help but feel for them as they seek to navigate round our lives, dominated as they are by this huge mountain which refuses to be cast into the sea. How much do they talk about the holiday they are so looking forward to?

How much can they say about what they hope to do when they arrive? They are our friends and so the last thing they want to do is rub salt into our wounds. Thankfully, since they have been such a major part of the journey, talking about natural things can be, surprisingly, quite natural. And genuinely, you are pleased for their happiness, since now more than ever you realize that it is not to be taken for granted. You learn to take pleasure from other people's happiness and allow it to be an antidote for your own pain. After about fifty minutes, Lesley has had enough and it's time to leave. 'I really love you,' she tells Caroline, as we walk from the door, and she means it.

Wednesday 5 June 2008
It's my dad's 70th birthday today and we will celebrate tonight with a little meal, glass of champagne, and a surprise present of a day trip on the Orient Express which, along with my brother Andrew and his partner Sandra, is a present from us for my mum's 65th and their forty-fifth wedding anniversary which all falls in the same year.

I heard back from Jeremy today – he emailed:

Dear Stephen,
Thank you so much for your letter. All three of you are often in my thoughts and I cannot explain how much I admire your family. I am so relieved that Lesley is able to access good care close to home. Please call any time – evenings are best.
    Warmest regards to Lesley.
      Jeremy McMahon

Friday 6 June 2008
The house has less people occupying it this morning since last night my parents went home for a few days

and David has set off for work. Once again I was up late last night reading till about 1 a.m.

Once I'm up and showered I go and wake up Charlotte, who has not been able to get to sleep until very late over the past three nights, which usually means a grumpy little girl is going to emerge from her bed. I'm gentle with her, and slowly she wakes. I help her to get dressed and washed, pop to give mum and nana a kiss, then go downstairs for breakfast.

'Are you positive you don't know when mum is going to die?' she asks as we get downstairs.

'No darling, I really don't,' I reply, not wanting to take the conversation any further, conscious that if we do it might upset the school routine. When breakfast is finished we make our way to school, and as we arrive in the playground she is anxious and starts to cry. 'I don't want to go to school. Really Daddy, I really don't want to go to school.' I gently ignore her tears, stay firm and reassure her that she is going to be fine and I will be there to collect her later. As she walks in line she is still in tears as I hand her over to the class teacher. However hard it may be, I come away confident that her school routine is one of the most important parts of her life at present. We don't want to rock any more boats on her choppy sea of life.

When I arrive back home, Val is into the established routine of morning medication, and after Lesley has taken it, she settles down to rest. I sit beside her as she sleeps and read *The Enduring Melody*, by Michael Mayne: the diary of how he handled his own journey of cancer. I do want to read it, don't want to read it; don't want to pick it up, yet can't put it down.

Saturday 7 June 2008
This morning Charlotte is off to plant flower boxes for Nottingham in Bloom with her Brownie group and I've

volunteered to run some lifts, so we're up early and on our way by 9 a.m. When we arrive I go off to make a call to Jeremy McMahon. Before I call, I know there is little he can suggest but, from past conversations, talking with him helps. His knowledge and ability to process what I am witnessing is a measure by which I can gauge what is happening. With Jeremy, it's as if I am talking with someone who has already been there and so is in a position to shine light into my darkness, even if the prospect of seeing is scary.

We spend about half an hour chatting on the phone. I'm walking in the park and he is out with his children, and occasionally he interrupts the conversation to bring some order to their playing, which I can hear as we talk. The joy of their shouting contrasts heavily with the depth of conversation we have quickly entered into as we discuss Lesley's present condition: Jeremy readily aligns my description of her symptoms with the progression of her disease. He explains that the hole I see in the roof of her mouth is tumour erosion where the blood supply to the area has ceased. 'Yes, Stephen,' he says, 'you can expect that erosion to continue. On a mass that has progressed to the extent of Lesley's, a 5 per cent increase to the whole represents significant growth.' I'm clambering after his words and shaking as I hold the phone, trying to absorb the implications of what they mean. What he calculates as good maths I see as emotion, pain and suffering in the life of a woman with whom I have spent the last two decades of my life. 'It's terribly cruel, Stephen, the way the cancer begins to infiltrate the critical structures of the head, I'm so sorry.'

I've met many consultants and doctors over the years of Lesley's illness, but none have matched the empathy of Jeremy. He has mastered not simply the technical competence of his profession, but also the pastoral ability to deliver the information in a warm and unrushed manner. Even bad news tastes better served warm. And you don't get much warmer than being given the private number of a consultant who offers you to call him at any time.

Before we hang up, he reiterates his admiration for us as a family in how we have dealt with the situation we have faced: 'I'm full of admiration for both of you,' he says. Strangely, it helps. We may have lost Lesley's health, but at least we have kept our dignity. Maybe it's about control, maybe it's about character; whatever's the truth, it is good to know the cancer cannot conquer everything.

Later that afternoon we have a visit from our friends, Martin and Katie, and their three children. After a cup of tea and quick chat, the children are off to play in the garden, soon followed by myself and Martin, leaving Katie and Lesley to chat in the lounge. It's not long before tears are being shed, and periodically I pop my head round the door to check things are OK – that both of them are handling the emotion which has now taken centre stage in our home. They are both upset but handling things well, so I leave them to return to the garden.

It's a glorious sunny day and we enjoy the latter part of the afternoon outside, as the children ride bikes, play games and take turns on the swings. Between our times of being dads, we both chat, Martin asking how we are, offering their support and help. No one seeing Lesley for the first time in a few months can help but notice the deterioration in her body – she is looking frail. Once the games come to end we go back inside, their initial short visit now well extended beyond tea, and we decide to order pizza before they go. The last hour ends up being a little fraught and maybe I ought not to have suggested the pizza, but it's a small price to pay for an otherwise wonderful afternoon. We could do with more times like that one.

Sunday 8 June 2008

Yesterday took its toll and left Lesley not feeling well enough to go to church for the service. But it was still a price worth paying.

Later that afternoon we all go off in the car for a little trip out, and finish up in one of the local parks followed by a call to McDonalds. Lesley can't eat out any more and wants to sit it out in the car. We object, saying she ought to come with us. We win. As we walk across the car park she says to me, 'I wish you lot could just know what it feels like to be in my position; none of you understand. Why couldn't you just leave me alone to sit in the car?' No we don't, we simply don't understand how she feels.

Monday 9 June 2008

I have a call first thing from my friend Andrew Fantom. 'Can I pop by and see you both?' he asks. 'Nothing cryptic,' he explains, 'just thought I'd pop by and say hello.'

He arrives at 1.30 p.m. and we go off to the summer house to chat. Not long afterwards he tells me his reason for coming. He's been to a revival meeting down in Dudley, had hands laid on him, and feels he may have a divine impartation to pass onto Lesley; what do I think?

He's obviously a little nervous; he has wrestled with the idea of coming to see us for the past ten days but can't get this idea out of his mind. He's not spoken with anyone else about it, and never normally prays for people in this way. 'Cancer is the modern day leprosy,' they have told him at the meeting, 'and God wants to cure cancers like he used to cure leprosy.'

Andrew is a genuine guy, and he and his wife Tracy have been our friends over many years, so I agree to prayer. A little later, Lesley comes to join us and I explain the reason he has come to see us and ask how she feels about prayer. There is no problem, so a few minutes later she stands and we join together in offering prayer and any impartation that Andrew might have received. Once again we have opened an opportunity for God's power to be released.

Afterwards I am happy with how the situation has been handled. I have set aside my own scepticism of what this new revival is all about, and quietly and hopefully trust for good to come from it.

Tuesday 10 June 2008
Today I read Psalm 6. 'Be merciful to me, LORD, for I am faint; O LORD, heal me, for my bones are in agony.' He goes on later in the psalm to write, 'I am worn out from groaning; all night long I flood my bed with weeping and drench my couch with tears' (vv. 2,6).

The Psalms appear to carry as much lament as they do praise – maybe that is the reason we draw on them so heavily to bring comfort to the oppressed.

My own reading of the Bible has been somewhat sporadic over the past few months since my appetite to pick it up has been lost. What would have once been a daily commitment has of late been a weekly chore – it simply lost its appeal. I know I will get back to that place, but it is taking longer than I'd wish. That and prayer have become vacant disciplines in recent months, a confession that I don't like to make, but a true one nonetheless. So beginning to read the Psalms again does bring a sense of connectedness. David pours out his heart to God in a frank and honest way. In fact, he is brutally honest and sees no wrong in it, and neither do I. If the Bible is not to be taken literally, as I have been taught to believe, then a new form of interpretation is required, and maybe that is part of the journey I now face.

Having departed for a while from the Scriptures, my
appetite for reading is nonetheless still keen and my
interest in the diary of Michael Mayne has continued. I
can only presume from certain sections of his reflections
that he is liberal in his theology, and wonder if I might
be transforming into one myself! I discovered real light
in reading a section that several years back would have
left me stumbling in the darkness:

> To speak of God as all-powerful is confusing if that con-
> veys a sense of one who directs and dictates our lives,
> and whose nature is so volatile that he creates floods and
> earthquakes and tumours because he is angry or dis-
> pleased with us. That would make a nonsense of the core
> Christian belief that the most accurate definition of God
> is Christ crucified, the ultimate symbol of dislocation
> and shared vulnerability. Rather, he seems to be a
> Creator who, in an act of divine self-limitation, relin-
> quishes control over creation, allowing it and its crea-
> tures to be self-creative as we seek for beauty and good-
> ness and truth, and struggle to learn the meaning of the
> stewardship of nature, the power of reconciliation and
> the language of love. The result is a world in which
> much is allowed to happen that is far from being in
> accord with God's beneficent will.[21]

Thursday 12 June 2008

Val and Dave went off early this morning, but not before
having a further session last night as Lesley expressed
her concern about being cared for whilst her mum was-
n't here. My lack of empathy is clear in her mind during
these conversations, and compounded by the fact that
when she came to sit upstairs last night I chose to stay
down and watch the final of *The Apprentice* – a clear sign
in Lesley's mind that I would prefer to put such things

before her. Once this idea is birthed it tends to spiral downwards into a mini onslaught that leaves my character somewhat assassinated. I'm discovering that during these times it is really important not to react, but to stay calm and remember the context of pain and hurt out of which she speaks – she has to vent her anger, and as her husband I'm often the target. Where else can she go? But it doesn't get any easier, especially when we are all bumping along at the bottom of our energy and emotions.

At 8.40 a.m. Charlotte and I go off to school, and on the way into the playground she asks again if I know when her mum will die. 'No, I don't, darling, I really don't know.'

'It's alright to guess, Daddy,' she tells me, 'because a guess is not a promise.' She then goes on to explain that if I made a promise about when her mum would die, then she would have to die at that time since a promise cannot be broken. Anyhow, no sooner are we finished with that little conversation than we are taking a look at the dinner menu, which is attached to the main door with Sellotape. Today she chooses spaghetti bolognaise and garlic bread. I leave quite fancying stopping for dinner myself. We then get in line and off she goes with a smile: today she is going swimming and she's happy with that idea.

When I get back home it is straight into the medicine routine so that by 9.30 a.m. Lesley can be settled down for a further sleep till about 11 a.m. when it will be breakfast. Normally her mum would take care of the medication, but today she has gone off to get some physiotherapy on her foot at Chesterfield. Morning medication consists of paracetamol dissolved in water along with gabepentin, a nerve painkiller. Afterwards she takes 10 ml. of Kappera liquid in a syringe to help control any potential fits. She then settles back down for a rest. I sit beside her bed, eat breakfast and then read.

At 11 a.m. I wake her up for breakfast: Weetabix with milk, and a cup of tea. We then plan to get her up and off she goes to the bathroom. Not long afterwards we are downstairs, but she's still not feeling well and so I sit with her on the settee and she drops off to sleep – and so do I! About 1.15 p.m. I wake and eat lunch and then we get up. At 2 p.m. it's more medication, and afterwards Lesley fancies something soft to eat. We go off together to the local shops, pick up a small quiche and bring it home. She eats it and then I prepare to go and pick Charlotte up from school. At 3.40 p.m. Lesley and I have an appointment with the head teacher from Charlotte's new school – she has invited us to pop by and meet the lady who will be her new class teacher.

As we walk into Reception, we are greeted by Mrs Austin, a tall, slim lady with long blonde hair. She has an infectious smile and greets us warmly with a confident, yet softly spoken 'Hello'. She then introduces us to Mrs Welberry, an older staff member whom I consider may have been chosen as Charlotte's teacher because of her age and maturity. She is the longest standing member of the staff team. We are then given a tour of the school and shown what will be Charlotte's classroom, a nice bright room, with windows to both sides and a view over the playing fields. The school has a warm, confident feel to it, with excellent displays positioned round the majority of the corridors. After the tour, we are taken to the head's office where we sit down and discuss Charlotte's move. It appears to have been well thought through, and after twenty minutes or so of discussion we leave, feeling hopeful that things are being put in place to, in Lesley's words, 'undergird Charlotte's transition to Juniors'.

'I really hope to see you on Charlotte's first day,' Lesley remarks to the head as we leave.

After tea, I take Charlotte upstairs for a bath and hair wash. When we get back down, her mum's not feeling great and so is lying down on the settee. She promptly gets up and goes to lie down upstairs, having left instructions about Charlotte's bed time. After supper, I take her up and tuck her in with a prayer. I then go off to check on Lesley to see how she is – she's fast asleep. I go downstairs and ask my mum if she will sit in the room with Lesley whilst I sit down and read the paper and watch one of the Euro 2008 football games on the TV.

It's 9 o'clock. Lesley has woken and found I'm not there. I'm in trouble. 'Why didn't you stay with me? You could see I wasn't well, and yet you just went off and left me.'

'No, I didn't,' I reply. 'I asked my mum to come and sit with you.'

'But you weren't there; you just weren't there, when I needed you.'

I explain I was just downstairs watching a bit of TV to relax. It doesn't help.

We move on, and I get onto the bed to cuddle and comfort her, whilst listening to her worries and concerns. She has many. If it were me in her situation, I'd have more.

We spend the rest of evening in the bedroom, and finally settle down to sleep after her last medication of the day at about 11 p.m.

Friday 13 June 2008
Still struggling to read the Bible.

I'm not sure if Lesley is suffering some type of breakdown. She's been increasingly unwell over the past few days, but the illness is not simply physical. When she is not able to take breakfast easily and with the weekend in sight, I decide to call our surgery and request a GP home visit. They agree, despite my call coming late in the morning. Their support has been great. Lesley is not happy at my insistence on calling him, but once he arrives just after 1 p.m. takes comfort in talking about some of her concerns. A listening ear is some of the best therapy available to her, and his patience seems to help. The fact that not a lot else is on offer doesn't, and after he goes, she gets up and leaves the room.

Before he arrived I had suggested we got out of the house for a while. It's not until a few minutes later that I realize Lesley has packed some things in her bag – toiletries, medication, change of clothes – and I realize all is not well. Is it panic? Not sure. A breakdown? Maybe. Something caused by the tumour growth? Who can tell? Whatever the truth, Lesley tells me she can no longer bear to be in the house and wants to leave. We pack her stuff in the car and head off for a drive, not really having any idea where we might go. Over the period of our drive she calms down a little and after an hour or so we head back home.

As we drive back to the house, I spot Charlotte with my parents walking down the road, having paid a visit to the local supermarket. We all arrive at the drive at the same time, walk into the house and prepare for tea. What a strange afternoon it had been.

Saturday 14 June 2008
I get up and take Charlotte to the park with her new bike. We have a great time and she is learning to ride really well; I'm very proud of her.

Later that day, our friends John and Sarah Fahy call by and we go off to take the children to a big kids' event held in one of the large city churches. Charlotte really enjoys it.

It's made for a good day.

Sunday 15 June 2008
It's Father's Day. Lesley doesn't make church for the morning service, but we have planned a day of prayer and fasting for her, with public prayer to be held in the evening at 6 p.m., and she wants to attend. Preparations are made for it to go ahead regardless of whether we turn up, and when we do everyone is pleased. Prayer has been arranged in several stages by Helen Fearn, who has given real thought to how the night can best work.

Travelling to the event, having fasted myself for the day, is an odd experience. Will prayer change anything, I wonder? And I struggle to get my head round what we are doing – praying for Lesley's healing, without which she will die. Just bizarre. Totally bizarre. I start to think about whether I have taken the evening seriously enough. Should I have fasted longer, or more frequently, during the course of her illness? If we were going to mobilize prayer, should we not have done it more often, and sooner, when it would have been easier for God to heal, since the tumour was much smaller back then . . . a lesser job for God to handle? I can sense myself juggling inside a barrage of interacting and connected issues, and struggling to make sense of it all.

I think about one of my friend's comments that God can step in with a miracle right up to the last minute. I mean, is that right? Can God really do that, and does he? I'm wishing I'd asked for some examples, some non-biblical examples. We all know God did miracles in the Bible, but what about now? People talk about miracles with such flippancy, as if for the Christian they are a matter-of-fact part of our experience, but now I wonder if that's right. Is it really true? I feel like the man in the Bible who, when questioned by Jesus, replied, 'I do believe; help me overcome my unbelief!'[22] I, too, am that walking contradiction. I simply want an authentic faith, one that I can live, teach and pass on with integrity, that's all; and our life is challenging deeply my previously held positions. I conclude that I don't need miracles to hold an authentic faith, I just need clarity on how all this stuff pans out in real life situations – and if God doesn't act in direct intervention through prayer, then what is prayer? Am I becoming a sceptic? And does it matter if I am? There are so many questions and so few answers.

After the meeting has finished, I speak with a few people, thanking them for taking the trouble to come and pray. Lesley is not keen to hang round for too long, and neither am I. My twenty-four hour fast finishes at 8 p.m. and I've got a piece of tuna waiting for me at home. Later, as I sit down to eat, I'm left wondering if a miracle would have been granted if I'd extended my fast to forty-eight hours. How mad is that?

Monday 16 June 2008
Today I received an email from one of our friends at Charis:

Hi Stephen,
Words seem inadequate sometimes, but just to say that you and Lesley continue to be an inspiration. Charis is an amazing church and I am so blessed to be part of a loving family.

We all love you so much and if there is anything at all I can do, please do not hesitate to ask. My mum has just called to ask how it went last night, she will be praying also as are lots of her friends – Lesley has touched so many of our lives, especially us girls and we continue to lift her up and ask for that miracle to come.

Jo

This afternoon we had a visit from Nicola, the Macmillan nurse. We'd been encouraging Lesley to ask about the possibility of starting antidepressants. She is completely against the idea, since she wants to be fully aware of her emotions. Knowing Lesley as I do, I was against the idea too until recently. But things have changed, and the degree of heavy sadness she carries is horrible to witness. It leaves her deeply disturbed and chronically unhappy. The pain she bears is terrible and, now I agree, if there is something that might help carry her load then it needs to be considered. Anything that might bring some life to her days needs to be examined.

During the process of conversation, Nicola asks whether she is finding strength in her faith at this time. 'Oh, absolutely,' she replies. But even faith doesn't take away the real darkness which is wrapped in the truth that she is a 37-year-old woman leaving behind a young family. Antidote for that type of pain is not readily available.

After tea, we take a trip out in the car, but it's not long before Lesley is not feeling well and we are heading back home. We step in through the door and it's plain to everyone how poorly she looks, and she goes off to bed. I follow, take a seat in the chair and sit with her as she goes off to sleep. About an hour later, I head off downstairs for a drink.

Later her dad goes to sit with her and then she calls for her mum. She has increased pain in her face, leaving her uncomfortable but, more concerning, her mood seems to have changed. There is a vacancy in some of her speech, and although her comprehension is complete it's not

fully mature, leaving me worried. As the evening progresses she is getting worse. She knows where she is, but
something is not right. I'm sitting in the chair next to her
bed, holding her hand and smiling. Inside, I'm dying and
holding back the tears but desperate not to show it. 'I've
got a little girl, haven't I? A little girl . . . she is in another
room. Can I see her? I want to see her now.' All this talk
is very strange. This is not Lesley as I know her and I'm
struggling to understand what is happening. Is this just a
blip? She's had an extra dose of orimorph earlier for the
pain – is that causing this change? I really don't know.

We help her out of bed and lead her to the bedroom.
'My girl, my beautiful little girl,' she says as we walk
into Charlotte's room. Now I'm really worried. This terrible disease is taking her physical body; please God,
have some mercy, don't let it take her mind too. We get
her back to bed and I go off to cry.

After getting to bed well after midnight, I'm woken
by her dad at 3.15 a.m. 'Lesley is having a fit,' he says.
'She's asking for you.'

About half an hour later, I'm back downstairs to get
some sleep. Rest has come to us all again.

Wednesday 18 June 2008
Lesley woke with a further fit this morning. Their fre-
quency at the moment is increasing. Often, they don't
last too long, but they are worrying at the time, since
there is little we can do outside of sit and support Lesley
as it passes. She's also spending longer in bed in the
mornings.

Today's major task is a visit to school to see Charlotte
perform in the Caribbean Parade. At 12.30, Lesley is still
in bed, and tentative suggestions are made that she may
not be well enough to go. After these conversations have
persisted for a half hour or so, she pulls herself up in

bed, musters her strength and says to us, 'Listen, I am going to school even if I have to drag myself there. I will go and see Charlotte in her parade.'

With that matter clearly settled it's not long after that she is up and dressed and preparing to attend. We set off early so as to get ahead of the crowds, and when we arrive, the gate to the playground is still locked. We pop off to Reception and as soon as Jenny Bradbury, the head teacher, sees us, we are welcomed to take a seat in the staff room and wait for the others. Kindly, she reserves the bench outside for us to sit on. At 3.10, the children arrive and show off their costumes as all the proud parents look on with excitement and joy as they perform in front of us.

After tea I meet our friends Caz and Steve and enjoy a nice drink in a local pub before going back home to have coffee with Lesley in the summer house. During our conversation, we chat a little about the now branded 'Lakeland Outpouring',[23] and I explain to them some of my dilemmas with the whole so-called revival. Later that night, both prompted by our talk and stirred by an article in *Christianity* magazine,[24] I decide to write a letter in response to a request made by the editor to send him reactions to this latest proclaimed revival. I wrote:

Dear Editor
Searching for Truth . . .
In response to your article, 'A Fresh Outpouring?' and your invitation to present our views, I pondered whether to write. What's my reaction to the 'Lakeland Outpouring'? Well, at best, I think it is mixed. For me, it's a tough one, compounded by my wife's terminal cancer and then further by my 'position' as Pastor to a local Church. She's only 37, and a month ago I had to sit down with our 7 year old daughter and explain to her that mummy was going to die.

I think my reaction is mixed because our needs are so great. If ever healing was needed in our family it's now. Yet I find myself tossed between scepticism and hope, with faith, that ingredient which releases God's power, dwindling behind desperately trying to keep up. I want to believe it, of course I do. I'd love to think the answer to our problem lies in an airport hanger and is simply a plane ticket away, but I'm just not sure. That's the problem with illness, the issues become so personalised, so inwardly focussed.

For me, the difficulty is not with Bentley, his style, tattoos, his 'Bam' or his 'Booms'; no, it's simpler, and much more basic. My quandary: Is it true? Do people like my wife with terminal cancer that has taken one eye, her taste, smell and shows the physical evidence of breaking through the soft palate of her mouth actually walk into these meetings, or put hands on a TV or computer and get healed? It's not a trick question, or even a cynical one. It's a yearning for the truth. The thing that Jesus promised would set us free.

I understand it's much easier to be objective when you are not emotionally involved, but the problem with Christendom nowadays is that we are involved. We're all involved, like it or not. Modern media, the internet and publications like your own, make it our business whether or not we want it. No bad thing, maybe. But as we all know, to he who is given much, from him much is required. And how we play out God's power within the context of 'revival' has massive implications not only on the well, but also the sick – those amongst us who are left vulnerable because of illness. Should I protect my wife, her emotions and fears or present her with another healing scenario? It's a tough call, hence my mixed reaction. I don't want to close the window of opportunity, I just need a little help in being led to it, lest it slams in our faces and we are left picking up yet more shattered pieces.

When I spoke with my daughter a month or so ago, I didn't have the dilemma I have today. Back then, Florida was a holiday destination, a place where Mickey Mouse lived not a hotspot for divine healing. Now, however, things have changed. 'Have you heard about the Florida Revival?' people ask, the intimation being maybe this is God's answer to our situation.

So what help can the Christian media give to those of us for whom good information is not simply a great read, but something more fundamental? Solid, honest reporting is I reckon the place to start and your article appears to go some way in this respect. Then we need genuine stories of healing. If good Christian journalism could take us by the hand to one or two case studies that cover not simply testimonies but also medically affirmed claims, it would help no end. If hundreds of miracles and healings are taking place, then solid verification of a good proportion of them should be easy to attain. If not, we need to be careful lest we lose integrity in our desperation to encounter the supernatural. Interestingly, in the same edition of Christianity you reported on Philip Yancey 'taking the double' in the Christian Book Awards for his latest work, 'Prayer – does it make any difference?' From my reading of the book his writing is a long way from the Florida experience and somewhat polarises the debate that such revivals raise. Is it simply faith that separates the two or something much deeper?

For my part, last night, I sat down to consider what shape my faith would take if a needed miracle was not part of it. Would it stand that test? Would it crumble under the pressure? Would it lead me from Pentecostalism to Liberalism? Or take me down some other road of which I'm not even aware? Tonight, some friends told me a couple who lead a large Church in our city have just returned from a trip to the 'Lakeland Outpouring'. Tomorrow I will go and seek out their counsel. I want to remain open minded and warm hearted and maybe after their visit they can help.

Now all I need to do is to decide if it's right to send it.

I felt a warm connection as I prayed before I slept. It's a long time since that happened. I slept really well.

Friday 20 June 2008
It's late and I'm exhausted; I was sick at dinner time with stress. It must be that Friday feeling, since it happened last week too.

We both attended Charlotte's new Junior School for a talk on how it's run and what to expect. Afterwards I walked down to pick Charlotte up from Infants with Lesley and my mum.

This evening was Charlotte's Promise Evening for Brownies. It went really well and Lesley managed to attend. It had been a bad start to the day but finished up a little better.

Saturday 21 June 2008
It's Midsummer Day and raining! Charlotte and I go to town to get an engagement present for our friends Dan and Danielle. When we get back, I go off for a couple of hours to a leaders' meeting to listen to Gary Clarke, Senior Leader of Hillsong Church in London. Lesley is not happy and sends a couple of texts saying so! I decide it's best not to stay for the whole afternoon, and go back home. When I arrive, she's still not happy.

Later, I prepare to go to the engagement party with Charlotte. Her mum says she doesn't want to come, which is part of the truth. The other part is she feels neglected by me for going out so much today when she wants me to be there, so I get a call at the party whilst I'm talking to someone. I miss it first time and then ignore it, till I have finished my conversation. She keeps calling, eight times in all. I finally answer and she wants to know why I didn't want to take her, and how I've caused her to miss out on something she would have loved to attend.

We get home just after 10 p.m. and get Charlotte to bed before getting ready ourselves, which is when it all goes a bit mad. Lesley blows her top, as an expression of her madness towards me leaving her out of things for the day. Then she blows her top at her mum for getting onto her when trying to help her calm down. After about half an hour we've all ended up downstairs to get some semblance of order before going to try to get to sleep. Charlotte sleeps through it all, and for that I am thankful for small mercies.

After everyone is settled down I go to the bathroom to be sick, and then head off to bed.

Sunday 22 June 2008

Today has been better. Lesley seems to have been more settled in herself, and we spent more time together which obviously helps. Although she didn't make church, we did get out after lunch with Charlotte and Val to a retail park, and it appeared to offer some therapy. After tea, Lesley and I went for a drive, got back and settled down for the evening; then we all went off to bed. Tonight, I'm sleeping in the spare room, whilst Lesley has her own hospital bed and her mum and dad sleep in our bed.

Before getting to sleep, I read a few articles from *Joy* magazine,[25] and especially those related to the Lakeland

Outpouring where, apparently the miracles continue to flow. It contrasts heavily with my other nightly reading from *The Enduring Melody* by Michael Mayne, where miracles are dealt out more sparsely. I could still really do with the former but seem to be dealing with the latter, which is both confusing and disappointing. Not least since I recently met someone who told me they had a friend who watched one of the Todd Bentley meetings and, at the time of prayer, hugged the telly and got healed. Some telly, I thought.

Meanwhile, back in the real world.

Healing talk and revival encounters have been reduced to only two this week. Some kind person sent us a healing CD with music with Scripture being read for us to play. And a further person checked we had done all the 'background' checks in the family history to ensure nothing was hindering our prayers. I managed to tick both boxes, so clear on those fronts.

Finally stopped reading Mayne's book for the night with the quote from his friend, Ronald Blythe:

> I have tried to imagine what [your illness] could have been like, for there is no greater chasm than that which exists between the sick and the – so far as they know – healthy. Imagination cannot bridge it, though love might now and then take a flying leap towards such suffering.[26]

I went to sleep thanking God for such love.

Monday 23 June 2008
In today's psalm I read, 'The LORD is a refuge for the oppressed, a stronghold in times of trouble. Those who know your name will trust in you, but you, LORD, have never forsaken those who seek you.'[27] That's encouraging to know.

Healing Revival Update . . . I received a further text today encouraging us to watch *God TV* since the person believes Lesley could be healed as a result of it. Not sure whether to be encouraged or enraged. People's perception of the miraculous leads them to believe in all sorts of weird and wonderful things. Like telly-hugging for example. Thank God for flat screens, I say; at least it makes the process a bit easier.

I'm still struggling to get my head round all this revival stuff. But it has to be said a lot of bona fide people are now into it, so I must exercise some form of restraint in my opinion. It just all seems a bit out of place. I mean, why do all these revivals have to be in the States that has one of the highest GDPs in the world, and where such a high proportion of people already go to church? Why not Mozambique or somewhere like that? It just seems all so convenient and not a little disrespectful to the poor who can neither afford the telly to watch it nor the plane ticket to attend. Still, it has to be said, if I genuinely felt Lesley could be healed by attending, I wouldn't let the money for the ticket stop us going. How's that for hypocrisy!

A minister friend called this morning, and he wanted an opinion from me on a matter. It was a really pleasant surprise to have someone asking for my opinion rather than enquiring how Lesley is and how we are doing. For those few minutes it felt great to be normal again, to know that someone can talk to me outside of illness, that my opinion still matters – a wonderful feeling.

Later that morning I went to Hayward's House, the specialist palliative care unit based at City Hospital, for some complementary therapy which felt very relaxing. It's one of the perks of being a carer. Nowadays people are much more switched on to the fact that those who care for a loved one need support too. However, I'd not realized when I booked the session how I would feel attending, and so when I arrived my emotions caught me off guard, and I found myself quite tearful as I walked down to the entrance, realizing where I was. This, after all, is where people come to have a good death. My wife could end her days here, and suddenly it all became very real.

Lesley's had a pretty horrible day and didn't make it to collect Charlotte from school. Tonight she was really emotional, and after a long conversation in which I examined my own attitude towards both her and the illness, we went off for a drive and sat for a while down by the River Trent. It was a beautiful summer's evening and children played by the river and fed bread to the ducks, which was usually pinched by the pigeons before the ducks arrived. We got back home about 9 p.m. and by 9.30 p.m. she was heading off to bed, and I went with her to help. Checking on Charlotte, we discovered she has been drawing more pictures of her mum and writing down what I had previously told her about the cancer. Lesley is concerned about the amount of time she spends doing it, and so am I. Neither of us wants it to become an obsession, but at the same time we want her to fully express her emotions and feelings and not suppress them in any way. We are trying to find the right balance. It's not easy.

Tuesday 24 June 2008
Got woken at 6.45 a.m.; Lesley was asking for me. Immediately went upstairs to sit with her. She was distressed for some time, mainly due to out of control pain, so I encouraged her to take some oramorph – which she did – and about fifteen minutes later she fell back to sleep. I went to wake up Charlotte and then showered whilst she ate her breakfast. We then set off and walked to school. It's a gloriously sunny morning.

When I got back, I relieved Val from sitting with Lesley and sat beside her. As I sit, I feel encouraged to read the Bible – which is such a relief. I read Psalm 10: 'Why, O LORD, do you stand far off? Why do you hide yourself in times of trouble?'[28] I'm so thankful that the Bible is about narrative, story, journey and process, and not formula. If it was about a success formula which some people seem to believe, this psalm would never have been included. But here it is, and it offers me such comfort to identify with its questioning. The Bible is such a wonderful book.

Went off for a meeting at 10.30 a.m. and got back for 11.30 a.m. when Florence, the district nurse, arrived. She spent an hour with Lesley and me talking over different issues, and finished with prayer before she left.

Just after 1 p.m., Carolyn, the vicar from the Anglican church next door to ours, arrives for a meeting and we go off to the summer house. She's cycled from Clifton to our home in Wollaton; I'm quietly impressed, and offer her a drink to cool down. After discussing work issues, she asks how Lesley is. I explain she's been telling how she feels stuck in a hole and keeps asking for help to climb out.

'I just don't know how to do that,' I say, weakly.

'Why don't you get in the hole with her, then?' she says.

Very good, these Anglicans, at looking for the other perspective: if she can't get out of the hole, then why don't I climb in and join her. Why didn't I think of that? What a very incarnational approach. One that embraces the idea of redemptive suffering, a concept mostly missed by us Pentecostals.

After she leaves, I take Lesley for a promised drive, by which time she is desperate to get out of the house. We drive over to the Ikea retail park, take a little look around, then head back home. Tea is soon prepared, and afterwards I sit with her whilst she takes some rest. Later in the evening I take her for another short drive. Meanwhile, I'm still thinking about climbing into the hole to join Lesley, and start questioning my actions and motivations in caring for her. I start by considering if I'm doing enough. Tonight, before I leave Lesley upstairs to sleep in our room with her parents, she begs me four times to take the bed I use in the lounge and put it in the bedroom next to hers. I refuse, gently, but I refuse nonetheless. Four times she begs me; four times I say no. Where is the tenderness in that decision, I wonder?

This idea of tenderness has been playing on my mind of late. I am wondering if now, for Lesley, tenderness is the only, or certainly most important, expression of our love, and is it found wanting? Earlier, as we were driving home, the words of the apostle Paul came to mind: 'If you have encouragement from being united with Christ, if any comfort from his love, if any fellowship with the Spirit, if any tenderness and compassion . . .'[29] There it is again, this word 'tenderness'. It's so strong, yet gentle. Tenderness can only be expressed when we are gentle and soft-hearted towards someone. It's one thing to show clinical care, a different thing altogether to show tenderness. And when you are facing what Lesley is facing, tenderness must feel like being bathed in the finest lotions.

As I settle to sleep, I quietly whisper, 'God, please help me to show tenderness' and I'm pleased to be uttering simple prayers as the last thing on my lips before rest.

Wednesday 25 June 2008
There is an immediacy associated with love that becomes clearer when times get harder. Tonight I tried to

take the moral high ground in asserting to Lesley the love I have shown to her over the course of the past five years during the anticipation, diagnosis, treatment and ultimate deterioration of her illness. It now stands for very little in light of present need, which is the whole point of love's immediacy – it must be expressed in the ever-present, otherwise love is lost; it has died. What is the value of saying, 'I did love you'? What matters is, 'I love you now.' From there, the way in which love is expressed depends on the situation in which it's placed. Love in our context is best – and maybe only – expressed through tenderness, which manifests in time, considera-tion, thoughtfulness and kindness. My own struggle to express love in that way may be a sign of my tiredness or self-centeredness; most probably both.

Earlier today, just after tea, Lesley suffered with a fur-ther bleed, the result of which was a large clot, or maybe piece of tumour or flesh, coming away from some place in the back of her mouth – possibly the back sinus area; it's difficult to know but was unpleasant to see. Thankfully it soon cleared up and in that respect she was fine for the remainder of the evening. Later, I went out with a friend for a couple of hours. I guess if I wasn't so selfish I'd have cancelled it.

Prior to sleeping, we all (Dave, Val, Lesley and me) sit in the bedroom and Lesley lets me know in clear terms what she thinks about my care. Her trauma continues: 'You don't have any idea how I feel,' she tells me. And then, using her thumb and forefinger to create a gap of about one centimetre explains, 'This is all that is left of the real me, the rest has gone, completely gone. Lesley Hackney or Martin (her maiden name) no longer exists; just a terrified, insecure and frightened person is left behind.' Her anxiety is almost tangible. I want to try harder tomorrow; she deserves better than this.

I prepare to leave and she asks why I've not prayed for her before I go. It's a fair question, and she swears at me, strongly. Good on her, I think as I snarl back and walk out of the room. A few minutes later her mum comes down to me and we have a chat. God knows, I am a pastor; if there is little else I can do, I can pray, and everyone thinks the same. Fifteen minutes later I go back to the bedroom. We both apologize and I pray, then Lesley prays, but with much more eloquence, sincerity and emotion. It's quite wonderful, simple, poignant and heartfelt. There is a connectedness to her prayers that brings me both sadness and comfort. Whatever else is happening through these times, the reality and importance of prayer and Lesley's walk with God is keener than ever. The irony is found in the contrast between her deep confession of her love for God, yet her apparent lack of peace in the face of fear. Perhaps this is where the human and the divine collide; perhaps here and now she is being made into the image of God, and what I am witnessing is simply the battle involved in that process.

Thursday 26 June 2008
Over recent times I have undervalued the importance of prayer in the context of illness. For too long I have viewed it simply in the context of physical healing, but this is very short-sighted and unhelpful. What if the place of prayer is not foremost to bring healing, but rather to make whole? This evening I prayed with Lesley again before we settled to sleep, and I felt a deeper sense of connection with God – not necessarily for me, but certainly for her. The vital place of prayer in her life to bring wholeness is massive. It does bring peace, a sense of divine presence and the potential of rest which extends much deeper than the physical realm.

Our prayers came off the back of what otherwise had been a difficult day, which started poorly and got worse. After lunch we set off for Chesterfield to meet John and Carol Begley, friends of ours. We'd not seen them for some time, and so the opportunity to meet was good. Afterwards we went off to see Dave and Val at their garage and then headed home, arriving back in time for tea. Lesley is struggling so much more with her emotions, and it is hard to understand the cause. Is it tumour growth in the brain, or simply stress over what she faces? I'm not sure we will ever know, but what I do know is: it's hard. I've noticed an unintentional change in my response to the oft-poised question, 'How is Lesley?' My standard response for some time was, 'Reasonable.' When she came out of hospital last year my response was, 'She's on the poor side of reasonable' as if to shift the enquirer's thinking down a few pegs. More recently I have described her weeks as being terrible, so as to allow for the deterioration in her emotional well-being in my response. After this morning and the hard time we had, when Carol enquired, I was about to reply, but she beat me to it, saying, 'Don't tell me, dreadful.' 'Exactly,' I said, 'and worse than dreadful.' She seemed to understand; perhaps years of nursing gave her the insight. Tomorrow I'm praying we can get back from dreadful to terrible; it would be an improvement.

Friday 27 June 2008
Doctor Mathoot arrived just after 12.30 p.m. for a scheduled visit arranged earlier in the week. He stayed for well over an hour.

Taking off his shoes before walking upstairs to the bedroom, he spent time with Lesley in a completely unrushed manner. Before he left, he asked to spend some time speaking with her alone. Fifteen minutes later, he came downstairs and sat on the settee whilst he wrote up a further prescription to add to her already long list of medication. She will now take 2.5 ml. of oramorph morning and evening to help with pain management, a small sedative to help aid a good night's sleep, and a new course of antibiotics, taken three times a day to hold any infection at bay. She's been running a temperature over the past five days or so which is symptomatic of an infection brewing somewhere. He also prescribed an artificial saliva spray to help ease her dry throat, which seems to be the main irritant behind her coughing so much during the night.

Later that day, Lesley told us what the doctor had been discussing. 'Why are you fighting with such fortitude, when many others in your position would simply give up?' he'd asked her.

'Have you got any children?' she replied.

'No, not yet,' he said.

'Well, when you have, you will know why I'm fighting,' she replied.

Some things have to be experienced in order to be understood.

Her brother, Mike, came this evening, and they spent time chatting whilst I was out with Charlotte getting a birthday cake for Nana in the morning. When we went to bed she told how she had spoken about her hope to see him in heaven one day.

'If they'll have me,' was his reply.

'Oh, they will,' she assured him. And before we settled down to sleep, I suggested that tomorrow she could get a copy of the Alpha book that explains what it means to be a Christian. She agrees; it will be one of our tasks for the day.

On driving to Sainsbury's earlier, Charlotte asked if her mum will be alive when she is 10. 'I don't think so,' I replied, as tenderly as I know how. She starts to cry, whilst trying not to let me see. 'I know what we can do, Daddy. I've got a good idea.'

Not knowing whether to be worried or comforted, I respond, 'What, darling?'

'Can you remember when I was 6 and you and Neil gave me the bumps for my birthday? Well tomorrow you can stretch me again, but stretch me till I am bigger and look like I'm 10. Then you can take a picture of me and give it to Mummy so she will know what I look like when I'm a grown-up. Then when she dies, we can put it in her hand, then she will have that picture of me in heaven as a grown-up and she won't miss out. That's a good idea, isn't it, Daddy?'

'Yes, Charlotte, that's a great idea. But we need to be careful how much we stretch you,' I reply.

Saturday 28 June 2008
I'm too exhausted to be bothered with writing today.

Sunday 29 June 2008
The household is reduced to five for tonight. Lesley's grandma went home this evening, having stayed over the weekend. Tomorrow we will grow back to seven when my parents arrive. Tonight we almost slept four to a bedroom, but in the end, I didn't, and so slept in the spare room. Not sure what to think of my actions. Lesley is desperate for me to sleep on the put-up bed next to hers. I've been refusing since it feels awkward, me sleeping in the same room as her parents. I mean, we all get on alright, but some things just don't feel right. I offered Lesley to sleep with me in the spare room, or for Dave and Val to use the spare room and us to have our bed back for the night. She refused that idea. The security of her parents is fundamental to her now, which leaves me

feeling grateful on the one hand and very inadequate on the other. Am I not capable any longer of providing what she needs? I'm not sure that I am which doesn't leaving me feeling too great.

We'd got to the place of me agreeing to sleep in the same bedroom after a mega debate over my love for Lesley or, in her eyes, lack of it. I know what she is saying and think she has a valid point, but I'm just not sure how love works in our lives any more. Love is still present, demonstrated in commitment, care and presence. But it does lack warmth and tenderness, and I guess I am the only one who can change that. I understand what Lesley and Val are saying to me; a lot of my statements and actions are cold and clinical. Lesley says that I wouldn't want her well any longer since I have already let her go. It's a very searching observation, and not one that I haven't considered myself. I wonder if in some ways I have let her go – seeing myself as nursing my wife through the end stages of life and therefore preparing for what is to come. I don't think it is conscious on my part, but I think in some respects it may be true. Is this what happens to people in my situation? I guess it may well be.

The earlier love debate was centred on the fact that the GP had suggested some respite for Lesley at Hayward's House. Since the suggestion was made on Friday it has now become clear I am the only one not to have told her she ought not to take it if she doesn't feel comfortable with the idea. So now of course it looks like I am the only one who wants her 'out of the way' for a while, which obviously doesn't help. It's a really awkward situation; I mean, how can you ever suggest respite care for someone without at the same time insinuating you want a break from them? And how could you want a break from someone you love? I feel a little like the goalposts have slightly changed from some previous conversations, but that's OK. This is tough on everyone.

I've been feeling really emotional at certain stages over the weekend. The first came after looking over *OK* magazine that Grandma bought with her. It had pictures of Wayne Rooney's and Coleen McLoughlin's wedding. I imagined Charlotte's wedding in the future; it made me sad to think her mum won't be there, and I imagined what that day might be like without her. Not really sure why I have to punish myself with such thoughts, but don't seem to be able to help it. Then this morning I woke up hearing Lesley coughing, and started to cry. I was just coming out of sleep and of late I've been troubled in the early hours of the morning, disturbed by dreams of impending loss. It really freaks me out and scares me. I'm glad to have woken up properly so I can take charge over some of those emotions. Have to say they are very strong and real when they come, and have the power of a large wave hitting you on the beach when you least expect it.

Monday 30 June 2008
Lesley's temperature was 39C this morning, causing Val and I to glance at each other with slight panic. After which the rest of the morning got off to a slower start than usual, and when I returned at lunchtime from attending to some work, she was still in bed and notably poorly. The rest of the day proved little better, and in the end she stayed bed-bound throughout.

Nicola Jones, the Macmillan nurse, visited this afternoon. We went over Lesley's concerns which relate to the present infection and what needs to be done about it. In reality, little can be done outside of what is happening with a two-line approach with antibiotics. Nicola stayed for over an hour and spent a little time playing with Charlotte before she left. As she was just about to drive away, Lesley called for her in a panic, so she came back and went over some of her concerns again. In the end she tried to contact the GP for us, requesting that Lesley's present condition is fully assessed. He was not available but agreed to call us after surgery, which he did. I chatted with him and we concluded that the present approach is the right one, but left the possibility of a trip to neurology open – we would discuss the matter tomorrow.

With the medicine routine now tweaked, we need to ensure the new regime works.

I heard back from John Buckeridge, the editor of *Christianity* magazine, today. He would like to include my letter anonymously in the next issue. I think I will agree. He wrote:

Dear Stephen,
Thank-you for your email.

The integrity, faith, doubt and pain in your journey right now moved me to tears.

I can understand why you do not want me to print your letter but I wonder if we might publish it without your name and with some changes to the details so identifying you as the author would be very difficult? If you decided to give us permission I feel its publication would provide an important voice that should be heard amid the other comments and opinions. So often those who are not healed, are not heard, and yet amid all the healing testimonies we do need to acknowledge the hurt and disappointment – that is real life, real faith, in the real world – which *Christianity* magazine in its strap line claims to represent.

Beyond that I am totally inadequate to comment about your situation except to say that I have prayed for you and your family to experience God's presence at this most difficult time.

To close I will not publish your letter with changes unless I hear from you.

With warm regards

John

Tuesday 1 July 2008

We're just settling down to sleep when Lesley realizes I have given her an extra 5 ml. of Keppra liquid by mistake. It's 11 p.m. when this happens, which is when the sparks start to fly. The next hour would be funny if it were not so painfully real. As her mum often says, 'If you told people, they wouldn't believe you.' So this is my telling of the hour that followed.

'Stephen, how much Keppra did you give me tonight?'

'Ten ml.'

'But don't you give me 10 ml. in the morning?'

By which time the light is beginning to dawn and I realize I have given her the extra, but try to wriggle out and pacify her concerns without lying! Inside I'm thinking this could lead to major anxiety disproportional to the event, akin to setting off a nuclear explosion in the search for coal.

'Yes,' I reply, concluding that coming clean is the best policy and the quickest way to getting a peaceful night for all concerned. How wrong you can be.

What follows is a full-on anxiety explosion resulting in demands for doctors to be called to sort out the mess. I suggest we take a look at the medication leaflet. This doesn't work, but I continue anyway, shooting off downstairs to fetch it. I quickly skim the mass of tiny text highlighting every possible complication that might occur as if the manufacturers are more concerned about litigation and profits than they are medication and care. Finally, I get to the place where it states maximum dosage within a given period. I read it with a huge sigh of relief when I can see we are easily within recommended limits. I eagerly take it upstairs to tell Lesley. She demands to read it for herself, but she's not happy.

'Call a doctor, call a doctor,' she demands.

Both her parents and I try to reassure her, but it makes no difference at all. The situation is simply getting more and more outrageous and more and more out of control. Something is going to have to give, and it looks like being me. Her dad offers to call NHS Direct, but I go instead and make my way downstairs to locate the number. In no time I'm speaking to a pleasant lady who takes me through a whole list of essential security information and basic medical questions, which are standard procedure to everyone who calls the emergency out-of-hours GP. She takes her time, is very helpful and speaks to me as if she gets calls every night from a husband whose wife is desperately ill with terminal cancer. Once we get to the crux of the matter – that I simply need some reassurance about our earlier medication overdose – she responds wonderfully and, without any patronizing, listens to the help we need whilst at the same time bringing up Lesley's medical history and seeing we are on the fast track system which guarantees a call from the doctor within twenty minutes.

Ten minutes later the phone rings. 'Hello! This is Sue, the emergency doctor.'

Both of us know that this call is more to do with Lesley's anxiety than any concerns over an extra 5 ml. of Keppra fluid, but she also knows that these issues are very real when someone is seriously ill, and so treats the call with the sensitivity it deserves. After a brief conversation she offers to reassure Lesley by speaking to her personally.

After a few minutes of reassurance the phone comes back to me, where we agree that her medication should continue as normal from tomorrow. Just before she hangs up the phone, the doctor says, 'Glad to be able to get you out of the doghouse.'

'Thank you,' I reply. If only she knew, I think.

For the next twenty minutes, the matter just gets more heated. Lesley is still mad. 'This is my life,' she insists, 'and you are just so blasé, you don't care.'

We could be in for a long night, so her dad comes over and sits next to her, trying to calm things down, but it's not working. I offer to sit with her. Then she demands I sit with her. The issue is now about control. Who's going to do what, for how long, in what order. Who's in charge here? Does it matter? We just want to go to sleep. But sleep is a long way off tonight.

'You go downstairs and come back here in fifteen minutes,' Lesley asserts. For the sake of peace, I reluctantly agree. The issue is no longer about simply power, but pride too.

At 12.10 a.m. I go back upstairs and sit with her whilst her dad gets into bed. After twenty minutes I get up to leave. 'You sit there!' she insists. I get back down, not wanting to push too hard and make things even worse. At 12.45 a.m. I get up again. Lesley shouts at me to sit down. I refuse. She shouts again and I get mad.

'Look,' I say, with my tone of voice raised, 'I'm getting very close to the end of my fuse, and if it goes off it's going to get loud and messy. I'm going off to sleep. Goodnight!' And with that I walk out of the door with no intention of returning. As I sit downstairs I can hear her talking for a while, but by 1.15 a.m. it's all gone quiet. Finally, it's time for bed.

Wednesday 2 July 2008

This morning I lost it. It's been very rare occurrence in my life that I have, and certainly never to the extent I did today.

The conversation from the night before continued this morning as soon as I stepped into the bedroom. It all got a bit heated and later, downstairs, I broke down and cried. 'I can't take any more!' I shout to Val. 'I just can't take any more.' I feel myself losing some sense of control. Shouting out more through my tears, I wail, 'That's it. I've gone as far as I can and I'm done.' I discover my body is suddenly tense and full of adrenaline . . . I pick up my hot cup of tea and throw it hard against the sink, smashing it to pieces. Val is now rushing to me and my mum is running downstairs. I've turned and with raised fist, smash it as hard as I can into the pantry door. Once, twice, three times.

'Stephen, Stephen!' my mum shouts at me. 'Stop it! Stop it!' she yells.

'I need to hit something. Move out of the way, I just need to hit something!' I shout.

Bang! Bang! Bang! Three more hits against the door.

'Then go outside. Just go outside!' Val says, her voice now raised as both of them try to hold me firm.

Storming outside, I head towards the shed. Bang! I smash the door with my hand. I walk up the path to the side of the house, panting heavily. All that's taking place is outside of my experience; what is happening to me? Turning round I storm back past the shed. Bang! Then I march off down the lawn, trying to bring my emotions under control.

After about fifteen minutes, I'm speaking to my mum, telling her that they will have to manage the day without me, and I'm off. I fear for my sanity if I stay around any longer.

Thankfully, I have an appointment booked at Hayward House for my second session of complementary therapy. As I arrive, I'm met by the therapist, Maureen, who's also a specialist nurse at the centre. As she begins to massage my feet, I pour out something of the last couple of hours and explain how I finally flipped.

Afterwards, Nicola the Macmillan nurse comes in to see me. She has been in touch with home and spoken with both Val and Lesley. Some type of agreement has been reached that Lesley will take some respite care at Hayward's House. I'm surprised with the agreement, knowing something of Lesley's thoughts on the subject, but privately relieved that some intervention is taking place, even if I don't have the confidence to think it will happen . . . and not even being sure I want it to happen, yet knowing something has to change.

'I flipped this morning,' I tell Nicola.

'Not surprised,' she tells me. 'You are all under enormous pressure, and I thought you would have lost it long before now.'

I take some time out during the afternoon, and after having coffee with Caroline at Sainsbury's Starbucks, I take a stroll along the canal. As I walk over the bridge that leads to the marina, I can hear a song playing from a local restaurant: 'I'm Still Standing' by Elton John. I start singing it heroically to myself. I arrive back home at 3 p.m. to find David has come home from work. 'I'm sorry,' Lesley says to me as I walk into the room. She's already said sorry on the phone before I got back, but wants to go over it again and again. And so starts an intense conversation going over various details of the night before. After thirty minutes or so, things calm down; Dave and Val come into the bedroom and we all sit together till Charlotte arrives back from school.

At 7 p.m. the GP arrives. He is the third professional to be involved today since Lesley insisted they all be called earlier this morning, and Dr Mathoot agreed to come after his surgery had finished. We have a long conversation, trying to agree a way forward. I state my position. I want more space, the pressure is too intense and I want time out, structured time to be away.

'You want to be away because you don't . . . because you don't love me and don't care,' Lesley insists.

'I think he cares too much,' Dr Mathoot responds.

'You would say that,' Lesley replies.

And so continues a lively conversation that ends with an 'agreement' for Lesley to stay at home, for us to get more help and support around the house, and for Lesley to take some diazepam to help relax her and take away some of the terrible distress.

'Lesley,' the doctor says, 'you have made all the decisions so far in the treatment of your illness, would you agree?'

Reluctantly she nods, and mutters a quiet, 'Yes.'

'Then now it's time for some other people to have a say in how things happen,' he says, 'time for others to form opinions on how things progress from here.'

Sunday 6 July 2008
The past few days turned out to be relatively quiet. Lesley is tired a lot of the time and struggles to get out of bed much before 1 p.m. But overall, things have been more peaceful; an attempt on everyone's part to bring less tension into the home which appears to have worked. Last night we all agreed to try our best to help Lesley get to church for the service, which meant waking her up earlier to allow necessary antibiotics to be given before any food is taken. We manage to achieve that goal, but nowadays 'the spirit is willing but the

flesh is weak'; her best intentions don't materialize and she misses the service.

It's perhaps as well, since at the end of the meeting one of the leadership group approaches to tell me she is leaving the church. 'I know it's not great timing, Stephen, but I feel God has told me it's time to move on.' She lists several reasons for her decision, and hands over a letter for me to read. I tell her I will read it later and we don't take too long together, since such conversations are always awkward. Before we leave, she explains how she put out a fleece as confirmation she was doing the right thing. Apparently, if I had not been in church it would have been a sign for her to stay. As it happens I've not missed a Sunday at Charis as yet this year, so that would have been unlucky, or lucky, depending on which way you look at it. 'Not great timing.' I recall her words as I go off to ponder the true value of understatement.

Charlotte and I get back home a little later, but Lesley has only just managed to make it downstairs with the help of her mum and dad, and not long after we settle down for some lunch. Later this afternoon her brother and his wife will be arriving with their daughters Kirstie and Terri.

They arrive at 3.30 p.m., but Lesley is sleeping on the settee and remains asleep for most of the time they are with us. About 5.30 p.m. we manage to rouse her and she sits quietly for half an hour. Before they leave, she musters enough strength to give the Alpha book to her brother, Mike. She is keen to give him something to read that explains the Christian faith. If she is going to heaven, then she is anxious her nearest and dearest would head that way too. He promises her he will read it.

Later, before Charlotte goes to bed, we play a game of Hangman which Nana bought her as a treat when we went shopping. She goes first, and chooses the word 'poorly'. I take a turn and choose the word 'smile'. She takes a second turn; this time her word is 'coughing'. I can now see how psychotherapists use role play and games with children to allow them to express their deepest feelings. The comforting thought is at least those feelings are emerging rather than submerging, and I hope that is a good thing for her future.

Monday 7 July 2008
Another email arrived today from a person offering to pray for Lesley's healing. I can't make up my mind whether it gets easier or harder to receive such offers as Lesley's illness progresses. He would like to visit with a friend since together they feel God has given them a ministry to encourage people. He wrote, 'I shared this with . . . . and we would both like to visit if you are agreeable, to bring new encouragement and stand in agreement with Lesley and yourself, for the manifestation of Lesley's healing which is already hers, according to God's promises.'

'Already hers . . .' Well, that would be nice. I'm just left puzzled as to why, if it is already hers, she has not thus far been healed. What is missing in the equation that releases some magical ingredient to allow healing to come? It's all so very confusing when you are on this side of illness. Several years ago it was so much easier: divine healing was a seamless part of the Christian message of atonement. The Scriptures that backed such teaching were a ready part of my own theology, but truthfully, even back then, I had nagging doubts about actually seeing some 'atonement healings' in practice. I wanted to believe it, like so many other people in church. Yet now, it all seems so far away; so removed from reality as to leave me wondering what it all means, how it fits into the agenda of God's kingdom and the landscape of suffering which so clearly frames our world.

In a respected Christian ministry magazine that arrived last week I read an article about healing that would have been much closer to my own position a decade ago. It stated that we need to look at sickness as if it was a snake which was climbing up our leg. If that occurred, we wouldn't just complain to others, we'd get up and shake it off our leg, yell, curse, and beat it. Now, of course, it sounds so simple – the only problem being, for us it hasn't worked. In fact, it has not even been close to working. As a result, I'm left pondering two things: firstly, am I profoundly wrong, and have I missed something along the way that could have changed our situation? Secondly, has the author been in a situation where this faith position has worked for someone with a degenerative and progressive illness like cancer, motor neurone disease or Aids? He goes on to write about praying for a friend with cancer, and how he continually declares healing, proclaiming the name of Jesus, until the cancer goes.

This position could not be further from that of Michael Hume, whose book I've just finished reading. He viewed his cancer not as a snake, but as a gift, something to embrace, to learn from, to be moulded and shaped by. For my part, I'm simply left wondering if it is only faith and conviction that separate the two views, or something else.

We had visits today from both Nicola Jones and John and Pauline Pettifor. This would be my third conversation of the day regarding Lesley's illness, and for the first time we discussed with Nicola Lesley's wishes at the time of death and beyond. She expressed that her only real desire was for family to be with her, but she was not too concerned whether that was at home or at

Hayward's House. I also raised issues regarding Charlotte attending her mum's funeral or Service of Thanksgiving. Lesley feels strongly that she is too young, and understandably does not want her to be there, worried that would be her last memory and something she would never be able to recover from. I am concerned that she has a proper opportunity for grief and closure. Nicola suggested that things should be explained to Charlotte, and she should decide for herself what she wants to do. At that point we left the subject alone.

Earlier in the day I'd been to see Jenny Bradbury, the head teacher at Charlotte's school. We chatted about Charlotte and her transition to Junior School in September. She told me how arrangements had been made for Mrs Finlayson, a teaching assistant that Charlotte is really friendly with, to attend Juniors a couple of times each week to help with her transition. It's a real comfort to know the extent to which they are going to help support us at this time.

Tuesday 8 July 2008
It's just after 11 p.m. and I've sat down to write a little before sleep. When I started the process of writing, it took the form of a prayer diary, a means of expressing brief prayers for Lesley to get well. Over time, it has become more a prayer/event diary, a way of recording the major events that shaped the journey of our life, faith and relationship. Recently, it has turned into an obsession, a form of therapy, a means by which I can record my own feelings, thoughts and emotions as they are tossed back and forth through the turmoil that has become life. I'm now at that place whereby it is necessary to write at least a few lines before I can sleep, as if through doing it I am redeeming something out of the

day, and recording it for posterity. Whether it would ever be right for others to read it is a matter for consideration in the future.

The television was on as I took my usual place sitting on the settee with legs resting on the put-up bed which would later be my place of sleep, and a programme called *Imagine . . . Anthony Minghella* was on BBC 1. It was a documentary, and one of the people interviewed caught my attention when he remarked that the thing with Anthony was his ability to take his pain and to make it beautiful. Immediately I reflected on our own experience in becoming sensitive to the redemptive theme of Scripture, how suffering and redemption are both unified in Christ and spilled out through the church; that God can make beauty out of ashes is the remarkable truth of the cross, and an ever-present source of comfort in our pain.

Lesley has been sleeping most of the day, and her frailty is startling to witness. Finally she managed to come downstairs at about 7 p.m., but by 9 p.m. it was all too much and she went back to bed. One really feels that the speed of her illness is gaining a serious amount of momentum, and it is harder to believe she will get back to a place of real mobility. I know her sights are set on attending the Ladies Night at Charis this Thursday along with parents' evening the same day. I'm not so sure she will make either, but the emotional disappointment will be significant if she doesn't.

The district nurse visited this morning and brought three further prescriptions from the GP. They all need to be kept in the house in case required; they look a little ominous.

After tea I find the courage to tell Lesley about the leader who told me she is leaving Charis. I was anticipating a stronger reaction, of her being upset . . . She isn't, not at all. She makes a few comments, and I agree completely with her observations. She wants to call the leader, but I persuade her not to and, after ten minutes or so, tiredness sweeps over her and she falls back to sleep. I look at her gaunt, worn out face and ponder just how massive her loss will be in my life. For all these years, Lesley's judgment on people matters has been one of her strongest gifts. Tonight simply underlines what I will lose when she is no longer with me, and pain wells up inside.

Wednesday 9 July 2008
When I get back from taking Charlotte to school, I go upstairs to sit with Lesley whilst Val goes off for breakfast. Ensuring someone is with her twenty-four hours a day has been part of our routine since she came home from hospital in late March. Today, I sat next to her bed and tackled a few jobs on my laptop. She has been confined to bed for the past three days and not been out of the house since Saturday evening.

After taking her medication she speaks of feeling really poorly, and asks if we could arrange for the GP to visit. I call to request a home visit. Dr Mathoot will be out to see her after surgery.

When he arrives at about 12.30 p.m., she is still sleeping and wakes just enough for him to examine her and speak about some concerns. As he leaves, he requests I speak privately outside the room. 'I think what we are seeing is simply the natural progression of her illness. Just make sure you keep her comfortable, and manage her medication as best you can. Let her eat and drink as she wants to and don't force her to get up if she is not able.' As we walk downstairs and chat at the door, he explains how he will inform the out-of-hours service and the ambulance service not to resuscitate Lesley should we call them out in an emergency. If not, then protocol would insist they have to attempt resuscitation, which would be unpleasant and unhelpful for everyone concerned – the last thing we want to end what has been a traumatic illness.

Not long before the GP arrives, I receive a call from Jill Finlayson from school. It's been Year 2's visit to Junior School today and she wants us to know that it has gone really well. 'Charlotte has been fine,' she tells me. 'She is really excited to be in Mrs Wellberry's class, and her friend Grace is in the same class.' There is a God in heaven, I think to myself, putting down the phone with a smile and sigh of relief.

When I pick Charlotte up later that afternoon, she comes bounding out of the door like a Labrador puppy jumping across fields of corn. The tearful little girl of last night has found her smile again, and it makes me feel really happy.

Friday 11 July 2008
Val has gone to get her foot checked out today, which means I will be around to care for Lesley. We start on medicines at 8.50 with a 5 ml. spoon of Oramorph, followed by 5 ml. of Oralclor and Metronizdole antibiotics, and then two paracetamol and one Gabepentin dissolved in water, then finally 10 ml. of Keppra liquid. This gets her through until 2 p.m. when it's another dose of antibiotics, two paracetamol and one Gabepentin. At 6 p.m. it's just Oraclor, two paracetamol and one Gabepentin, plus a 5 ml. spoon of iron, two Thyroxine tablets and 5 ml. spoon of Lactolose. At 10 p.m. it's back to Oramorph plus everything else that was included on the morning medicine cycle. It's a lot of medication.

Outside of taking medicine, Lesley sleeps most of the day, waking for a Weetabix at lunchtime and rice with mushroom sauce for tea. Otherwise she has a few brief conversations at different times, but suffering from chronic fatigue leaves her with little energy. At the end of the day, before I go off to sleep, she thanks me for trying so hard to care for her, and we pray together. I finally get off to bed at 11 p.m., feeling tired.

Saturday 12 July 2008
We have a full-on conversation tonight about death. How and where it will happen. The discussion is hard, long and with few meaningful answers outside of agreeing that, although Charlotte must not be fully protected from her mum's passing, she does need shielding from any potential trauma that might be associated with it.

The conversation turned this way since Lesley is feeling really low, and wonders if her end is close. For the rest of us, we have no idea, outside of realizing things can't go on indefinitely, and she is much weaker this week than last. But I think she could get a lot weaker than she is at the moment. Before I go off for sleep, she says she has God's rest. 'I have found God's peace,' she tells me, 'and it's sweet, real sweet.' I respond with mixed emotion, saddened and happy by her words. Whatever happens from here, my prayer has been that she would find the peace of God in her heart. Tonight she confessed to that reality.

Monday 14 July 2008
It will be seven days tomorrow since Lesley has been downstairs and her weakness appears to manifest in more sleep. We started medication tonight at 10.10 p.m. and finished at 11.45 p.m. Afterwards, we were all totally exhausted. How long we can sustain this level of care, I'm not sure; it is so relentless. Yet, still the truth is,

ours is the easy part of this process. Why ever should I complain? I'm not the one slowly dying of cancer.

Wednesday 16 July 2008
Lesley is still in bed and sleeps whilst I sit in the room with her. We've just finished morning medication that included a new drug which was like thick, sticky syrup that tasted of peach. We're now using oral syrup for paracetamol, which means there is less overall liquid for Lesley to drink which helps the process a little. On Monday, Nicola the Macmillan nurse came; yesterday it was the district nurse and today the phlebotomist[30] is due, along with the district nurse.

Later I'm off for my next complementary therapy appointment at Hayward House. Feeling pleasantly calm at the moment and peaceful, and that makes me grateful.

Tonight we are delivering cards for our 'Prayer Works' initiative. I picked up the idea from another church, but was encouraged to develop it ourselves in light of the importance of prayer in sustaining our own lives.

Thursday 17 July 2008
It was Charlotte's Leavers Assembly today, and I went alone and sat with the other parents in the hall. Not that I was the only lone parent there, but that didn't seem to matter. This was the first time Lesley had missed a significant step in Charlotte's life and the twelfth day since she'd stepped outside the house. It felt strange – even though she'd been so absent in the school runs over the past year – for her not to be there on this occasion. I'm not too sure how many others noticed or thought about the implications. I did. I thought about them as I walked to the hall. I thought about them as I glanced at Jenny,

the head teacher, who quietly acknowledged a small gift we'd sent her earlier that day. And I thought about them as I watched Charlotte walk down to the front with the rest of Class 4.

After a brief introduction, the children were into their first act and then into the song, one that I recall singing when I was at school.

> One more step along the world I go,
> One more step along the world I go.
> From the old things to the new
> Keep me travelling along with you.
>
> Chorus:
> And it's from the old I travel to the new.
> Keep me travelling along with you.
>
> Round the corners of the world I turn,
> More and more about the world I learn.
> All the new things that I see
> You'll be looking at along with me.
>
> Chorus
>
> As I travel through the bad and good
> Keep me travelling the way I should.
> Where I see no way to go
> You'll be telling me the way, I know.
>
> Chorus
>
> Give me courage when the world is rough,
> Keep me loving though the world is tough.
> Leap and sing in all I do,
> Keep me travelling along with you.

Chorus

You are older than the world can be,
You are younger than the life in me.
Ever old and ever new,
Keep me travelling along with you.

Chorus

'One More Step' by Sydney Carter – Reproduced by permission of Stainer and Bell Ltd, London, England.
www.stainer.co.uk

As I sat listening, the words of the chorus ran through my mind, 'And it's from the old I travel to the new. Keep me travelling along with you.'

I considered the old that was coming to an end for Charlotte and I. Not just a school, but a way of life, the loss of a mother and wife. The reality lay next to me in the vacant seat now taken by another parent, her life not known to me nor mine to her: in the casual conversation that normally passes the time of day about how sweet the children sang, how hot the room was, and how beautiful the service had been. I wanted to tell her why Charlotte's mum wasn't there. I wanted to tell her how she was lying at home, slowly dying. I wanted to tell her, but I didn't.

At the end, Jenny Bradbury stood to applaud the children for their time at school, for their hard work and for their future, for which she gave her best wishes. She quoted from the fourth verse of the hymn sung earlier:

Give me courage when the world is rough,
Keep me loving though the world is tough.
Leap and sing in all I do,
Keep me travelling along with you.

It felt like she'd said it for Charlotte and me. It felt like we'd need it.

Leaping and singing comes after courage, not before it. I need to remember that fact.

Friday 18 July 2008

Sarah arrived this morning at 10 a.m. She's a trained nurse and member of the Marie Curie organization, and had been booked as a sitter for the day to give some relief to us all. A tall woman in her mid forties, she's been doing this work for over ten years and was very professional and thoughtful. We chatted for a while before I went off to meet Dan for coffee. During the conversation she told how she'd lost her dad when she was Charlotte's age, and so I asked her numerous questions about how that had impacted her and how she came to terms with it. As Charlotte's father, I'm desperate for every piece of information and advice I can glean from others in helping to process Charlotte's life and circumstances to make her future as secure and rounded as possible.

Later, I went to collect Charlotte for the last time from Infants. Felt slightly emotional, but wasn't going to let on to anyone. In September she'll been starting Junior School. That's six weeks away, and only God knows what situation we will be in by then. Six weeks feels like a long time at the moment.

Saturday 19 July 2008

Charlotte has been asking me a lot of questions about dying again. The subject had been dropped for a while, but is now on the agenda in a big way. On the way back from town she wants to know if we can keep Mummy's body in the house after she has died, to remind us of her.

I try to explain it doesn't work like that, and when we die everyone's body gets taken to a special place. She goes on to ask whether the heart stays in her body, and the brain. I'm trying to reconcile in my own head the extent to which a 7-year-old can process death and dying, and how to meaningfully explain our belief in the afterlife.

'Mummy won't need a body when she goes to heaven,' I explain to her. 'So her old body gets left behind and we bury it. It's only the spirit, the real part of you, that goes to heaven.'

'Will we see her spirit going up to heaven, Daddy?'

'No, darling, we won't see it because the spirit is invisible. It's that part of us which we cannot see but does exist.' By now I'm feeling really inadequate in explaining one of the essential truths of our faith to my own daughter. What do I believe about death and what comes after? I'd better get my facts straight; I don't want to confuse her . . . or me either, for that matter!

Earlier in the day, I asked Lesley if I could see inside her mouth. Shining a little torch I took a look. The hole I'd seen previously gets bigger every time I look . . . I didn't examine it too closely, but it must be between a quarter to a third of the roof of her mouth. So I quickly took away the torch and said nothing. She's only eaten a biscuit and about six teaspoons of mashed potato in the last two days.

Before bed I pray with her, and as she settles down to sleep she apologizes for not being able to make it to church tomorrow.

Sunday 20 July 2008
Today I spoke at Charis. I took the theme from an earlier sermon called 'Aspects of Greatness', and looked at the unique contribution faith offers to life. There were

four elements to the message. Christianity is shown to
be great through: Outrageous grace, Inexpressible joy,
Inextinguishable light and Unconditional love. I frightened myself with the confidence with which I spoke,
wondering if my speaking is masking my true feelings.
Am I hiding behind a public persona? I wondered as I
left afterwards. How can you ever tell? All I know is I am
seeking to be true to my feelings and emotions, whilst
building life on what I have come to accept as truth. Of
course, I am encouraged to live in such a way if I take
the Bible seriously, which I try to do. One of the main
passages for the message came from 1 Peter 1.

Praise be to the God and Father of our Lord Jesus
Christ! In his great mercy he has given us new birth into
a living hope through the resurrection of Jesus Christ
from the dead, and into an inheritance that can never
perish, spoil or fade – kept in heaven for you, who
through faith are shielded by God's power until the
coming of the salvation that is ready to be revealed in
the last time. In this you greatly rejoice, though now for
a little while you may have had to suffer grief in all
kinds of trials. These have come so that your faith – of
greater worth than gold, which perishes even though
refined by fire – may be proved genuine and may result
in praise, glory and honour when Jesus Christ is revealed. Though you have not seen him, you love him; and
even though you do not see him now, you believe in him
and are filled with an inexpressible and glorious joy, for
you are receiving the goal of your faith, the salvation of
your souls. Concerning this salvation, the prophets, who
spoke of the grace that was to come to you, searched
intently and with the greatest care, trying to find out the
time and circumstances to which the Spirit of Christ in
them was pointing when he predicted the sufferings of
Christ and the glories that would follow.[31]

The idea of redemptive suffering has become one of the cornerstones upon which I've tried to build my life over the past few years. Without it, I can neither make sense of my own life or others'. Earlier in the week, I read an article in *The Independent* that says 4 billion people in the world go hungry and, of that 4 billion, 1 billion are living in total poverty. How do you make sense of that?

There has to be a refining associated with suffering that identifies us with Christ. Yet suffering cannot simply be a place of identification, it must also be a place of discovery, a place where Christ can be found. Maybe our lives are actually poorer for not having suffered, and although we ought not to look for it like searching out a certain ride at the fairground, when it comes, we must allow it to shape us in the likeness of him who was familiar with suffering'.[32]

Later that evening our friends Steve, Caroline (Caz) and Helen came round and we went off for a short stroll, followed by a drink in the summer house. Afterwards, as we walked up the garden, Steve stopped to tell me he felt impressed to say some words he felt God spoke to him in the service earlier that day. As I was speaking, the words 'do the work of an evangelist' kept coming to him. He felt he ought to tell me as something to consider. I don't know what it means, but I felt encouraged by what he said. The words are taken from 2 Timothy 4:5.

Monday 21 July 2008
It's a lovely, sunny summer's day outside as I sit typing in the bedroom and Lesley sleeps. The curtains are closed to protect her eyes from the brightness. It marks a clear distinction between a life that revolves round our bedroom and a world outside somewhere that continues to turn. I am able to escape into that world from time to

time, but for Lesley, life stops here. Nowadays, routines are built round medications, sleep, and further medication, a brief interlude here and there for food which is normally rejected and brief conversations that are, like I said . . . brief.

Sleep appears to offer the greatest sanctuary, a place where pain is left behind and the horrors of the days are given over to dreams which, I trust, for her are sweet, holding memories of better days when long summers were about the seaside and holidays, times spent travelling together in the car to Dorset or Cornwall; a life that was loving and happy with moments of fun, tenderness and joy. They all appear as distant memories now as I look at her worn-out frame devastated by disease, with hardly the energy to sit up in bed.

Each day gets harder, and as each one passes Lesley grows a little bit weaker; not able to even manage the commode without support. When she stands, her thin legs and the skin round them hangs loosely, like that of an old woman. The effects of the cancer are displayed in every part of her body. What this disease does to a person is horrible, simply horrible. And with each day comes the routines that accompany it, namely fitting in the long list of medication that's administered four times a day: 9 a.m., 2 p.m., 6 p.m. and 10 p.m. Tonight it took one and a half hours for Lesley to take her medicine as she cautiously sipped each spoonful to try to avoid irritating her cough. We sit her up using the electric mechanism on the hospital bed, and gently begin the long process. 'Just a minute, just a minute,' she says, trying to get herself ready. Each spoonful is carefully offered and slowly she tries to sip the medication off the spoon. Some of it slips down her throat, the rest dribbles down her cheek as her ability to control her mouth movement and swallowing action has been lost to the disease. It's painful to watch as she struggles with each medicine. First a spoonful of Oramorph, then two spoons of liquid paracetamol, followed by a Gabepnetin capsule which is split open and the powder mixed in a tiny amount of water and painstakingly swallowed. Then it's two spoons of antibiotic, and lastly a 5 ml. syringe of Keppra liquid, which is supposed to keep any fits at bay.

When we finally settle her down to sleep, I read to her from Psalm 62 which starts, 'My soul finds rest in God alone' and quietly I pray for that to be the experience for each of us.

Tuesday 22 July 2008

As I approach the traffic lights adjacent to Beechdale Baths on the Nottingham ring road, the phone rings on the hands-free: it's my dad. 'Come quickly, Stephen, Lesley is having a bleed.' I immediately pull over, turn round and head back home. I'd been on my way for my weekly de-stress at Hayward House, but that would have to wait. Five minutes later I'm back home and rush upstairs to see what is happening. It's the first time Lesley has had a bleed in over a month. Thankfully it's a mild one and after ten minutes things are calming down. I can see a small clot in the bowl, but compared to the last bleed it is only small and, with the panic over, we settle Lesley back down to sleep. I sit with her whilst Val goes off for breakfast. Before she dozes off, I take a look in her mouth to see if there are any signs that the bleeding might start again. I see evidence of the tumour everywhere inside, which is difficult to describe; just an eroded mess of diseased tissue, a large hole and areas of blood-coloured flesh. Not a pleasant sight and I'm left wondering how she is able to continue at all.

She sleeps the majority of the rest of the day, waking briefly round teatime and then again at 9.30 p.m. for medication. She has eaten no food and had no drinks outside of what she takes with her medication.

Wednesday 23 July 2008

Tonight I stood at the bedroom window watching the trees blowing gently in the wind as the sun fell peacefully on the day. Birds flew, and the sky turned a rich golden colour on this warm summer's evening. Apart from the occasional shouting from children in the distance, it was quiet. Behind me lay Lesley, sleeping in bed, drugged too much to sense her pain, and weakened by the activities of the day. Earlier she'd been fitted with a syringe driver – another threshold crossed in the process of dying in our western culture. All previous medication is now stopped. Paracetamol: gone. Gabepentin: gone. Keppra liquid: gone. Antibiotics: gone. All replaced by a cocktail of new drugs professionally mixed and delivered at 2 mm. per hour. There will be no going back to the old ways, no more fighting to get medicine in on time, no more struggling with that white plastic spoon which had become such a familiar item in the journey of care. The former things have passed away.

As I looked out over our garden to the trees and buildings beyond, my mind was taken back to a very different summer in 2004 when this journey began. I recalled standing in a different garden, that of Lesley's parents, and chatting with her father about our latest visit to the consultant in Sheffield. The storm clouds were only beginning to gather back then and, though anxiety lay low inside me, there was room for optimism. We were still a long way off a cancer diagnosis; our trips to hospital were investigative and filled with cautious hope. Today, it all seems like a very long time ago.

Now, as night begins to fall on another day, I wonder how many more days will be left for Lesley. I pray for a peaceful end, but it's not guaranteed. She's had two further bleeds in the past twenty-four hours with the real prospect of more to come, one of which could be fatal. Otherwise she might have a massive stroke to bring her time to an end, or she could simply fall into a deep sleep from which she never recovers. Her face is pale, her sleep disturbed by the occasional groan as she wriggles for comfort on her soft air mattress. The room is peaceful, save for the occasional whirr from the syringe driver as it delivers its dose, and I offer my prayers to the Father for his will to be done.

None of us holds jurisdiction over another person's life. Lesley's time is now in God's hands.

Tuesday 29 July 2008   1,257 days after diagnosis
Lesley died yesterday, 28 July 2008 at 1 p.m. She was 37. It was a peaceful death with her parents Dave and Val, Charlotte and I sitting round the bed holding her hand. Outside it was a glorious summer's day and the windows to her double room were open wide. It was calm and tranquil and felt like it ought to have been a holiday cottage rather than a hospice; that if you walked far enough across the grass verge you would eventually find the sea somewhere in the distance. But it wasn't, and as the morning passed her breathing started to change, becoming more laboured and intermittent. The early hours had passed quietly but now the telltale sign of a life drawing to a close dawned, and as the time approached 1 p.m. she took her final breath and passed away.

She'd been transferred to Hayward House the previous Thursday. Nicola Jones, along with her colleague, Fran had been scheduled to visit Lesley at 3 p.m., and when they arrived we chatted briefly downstairs. We'd all agreed that a move at this stage of her illness would be the best thing, and the day before, during a visit from Dr Mathoot, Lesley too had agreed with him that this would be the right step. Nicola was anxious for Lesley to express her desire. She sat for some time and asked if she would like to go. Naturally hesitant and not being able to communicate easily, she said nothing. I asked to sit with her. 'Lesley, Lesley,' I said, my voice raised more than Nicola's, 'I know you have heard what she has said. I need you to tell me you are as happy as you can be with this move.' It was never going to be an easy decision for either her or us, but we knew we had gone as far as we could with caring for her at home. 'Lesley, if you are happy with us taking you to Hayward House, then squeeze my hand twice.' Immediately she did; the decision was made and arrangements were put in place.

About an hour later, the ambulance arrived. We took the crew upstairs and they pondered over the best way to move her. 'How long is it since she was downstairs?' they asked.

'Over two weeks,' I replied.

'How far can she walk from her bed?'

'She can't,' I said.

This was not going to be easy. After further deliberations, they went off downstairs to call another crew for help.

They all stood outside the house, four crew members and their two ambulances, discussing how to get a sick woman weighing no more than 6 stone down a flight of stairs, with the least distress. As they were talking, suddenly Dave came down and shouted, 'She's up. She's got herself out of bed and is standing up.' Unbelievable, utterly unbelievable.

We all marched off to the bedroom and there she was, standing up, waiting for them to take her. They put a neck brace on, strapped her into their special chair, and manoeuvred down the stairs. At the bottom, she was put on to a stretcher and taken off to the ambulance. Val went with her as Charlotte and I followed in our car and Dave in his.

By the time we arrived, she was in her room and settled in bed. The trip had taken its toll and she was more awake than she had been for some time, but also in more pain. She indicated to us where the source of pain was and they administered further morphine to try to bring it under control. That would be the most conscious I would see her; from here on, drug induced sleep would be the only means to keep her comfortable and pain-free. It was now just a matter of time. All we could do was sit with her and wait.

Friday came and went with little apparent change. An acknowledgement through eye movement was all she could manage.

On Saturday, my friend John Fahy came over to see me. I suggested we pray for Lesley. He gently held her hand and I placed mine on her forehead. We prayed for God's comfort and peace. We prayed for her heart to be prepared for heaven. We prayed for Jesus to meet her there. They were measured prayers, and throughout Lesley acknowledged us with movement in her eye. It was deeply moving. Even now, with the reality of being there, it all felt surreal. Could I really be praying with her for the very last time? How did we get to this place?

When Sunday arrived, I was pleased she'd had a good night. Dave and Val had stayed over and slept in the room whilst Charlotte and I went off home to sleep. We arrived about 10.30 a.m. and the sister on duty had suggested we each have some time to be with Lesley alone. Charlotte had already asked to speak with her mummy and so we both stayed in the room and Charlotte spoke and told her how much she loved her. Afterwards, I stayed on my own. Held Lesley's hand and spoke to her. I explained how much I loved her, how special she was and how great we had been together. I made a promise to look after Charlotte and consider Lesley in the decisions I had to make as she grew up. I told her what a wonderful, kind and courageous person she was. And I told her that I would see her again in heaven. And then I cried. It would be the last time I spoke to her alone.

Friday 1 August 2008
Today we went to the Chapel of Rest to view Lesley's body. Nothing prepares you for that experience.

Monday 4 August 2008
In keeping with her wishes, Lesley was cremated at Wilford Hill Crematorium, at 10 a.m. on Monday 4 August 2008 and a Service of Thanksgiving was later held at the Christian Centre in Nottingham. Charlotte and I were dressed with matching white rose buttonholes. She wore a lovely pale lilac dress with matching shoes, and I wore a charcoal grey suit and tie with lilac flecks to match her dress. We held hands as we left the house and walked to the car, which led off slowly to the crematorium. When we arrived, we followed the coffin into the chapel and took our seats with Dave, Val and Grandma next to us. It was a short service and both John Pettifor and David Shearman set the tone, paying respects to Lesley, and to how the family had managed her care. John Fahy read from Romans 8:35, 'Who shall separate us from the love of Christ?' At the end we listened to 'Fields of Gold' sung by Eva Cassidy, and whilst it played I led Charlotte to the closed gates. We took one more look at the coffin, bowed, turned round and walked out of the chapel.

The Service at the Christian Centre started at 11.30 a.m. There were over three hundred people present, and Daniel Turner led the worship. We sang three songs in all, including the most important in my eyes, 'Be Thou my Vision, O Lord of my Heart'. Tributes were given by Jonathan Bentley, Caroline Hall and John Fahy, plus a time for others to share too. John Pettifor led the service and gave the sermon and Rae Galloway concluded with prayer. Charlotte read Psalm 46, one of her mummy's favourites. She was amazing, and her mum would have been so proud. I gave my tribute, a compilation of personal thoughts and reflections. I had it fully typed lest I should fall on the day, and the two Johns, Fahy and Pettifor, stood beside me as I read:

Thank you for coming along today to this Service of Thanksgiving. It means a lot to me and Charlotte, both sets of parents and our wider family that you have made the effort and taken the time to attend. Lesley was in the flesh and will remain in our thoughts and memories one of life's great people who graced this world with warmth, kindness and strength, and it's my honour, responsibility and privilege to pay tribute and express my thoughts as her husband, lover, pastor and friend.

It was early summer and the room was warmed by the sun as it shone through the windows brightening what otherwise was a clinical place. Behind us lay a dentist's chair, in front, a wood veneered desk complete with files, trays and books. At an earlier visit we'd been introduced to Jeremy McMahon, a consultant maxillofacial surgeon. He was a softly spoken New Zealander in his early forties and his manner was kind and in no way clinical, unlike the room in which he practiced. From the outset, he outlined his thoughts. The sensations Lesley experienced were a cause for concern; the question, to what degree? The year was 2004.

The synopsis was simple. The feelings on the right side of her face were either scar tissue from former radio-therapy, or something more sinister. The diagnosis was complex, none routine, and not without risk. We'd been with him for twenty minutes and the complexity of Lesley's condition was becoming clear. My heart sank. We exchanged glances; the journey of life was taking an unwelcome turn.

'Do you mind if I examine you?' Jeremy asked, his voice gentle but not without concern. She agreed, stepped into the examination chair, and he began. All the time Lesley held her nerve, kept her composure and cooperated fully, as if sitting for a regular dental check. I sat and watched, noting how she held herself and kept her head. I remember thinking, 'This woman is one remarkable human being.' And as the past had shown and the future would reveal, my judgement was not without reason.

Experience is to life what software is to a computer. It doesn't determine the look but it does define its purpose. You can't always see by looking just what you have on the inside. You don't always know what's on the inside till the outside is challenged. But what is on the inside matters – it matters a lot, especially when life gets tough, and for Lesley it was about to get tough; very tough indeed.

To my mind, Lesley had been an outstanding and beautiful woman long before our encounter with Jeremy on that Friday afternoon at the Charles Clifford Hospital in Sheffield. When we first met some sixteen years earl-ier, she struck me as a wonderful, kind and considerate person and, over the years, as our lives mingled into a unified oneness we became an inseparable team. I was edgy, forward-thinking and a little eccentric in my ideas. She was calm, competent and well-rounded. I was complete in my surroundings; she was complete in herself. She was a whole person, and it showed. She didn't need the approval of others to do what was right, and would not allow the disapproval of others to prevent her doing what she believed was right. Lesley was a woman of conviction, and I respected that.

Her ability to maintain her convictions led to many exciting times, especially when they clashed with my own. To have known her was to appreciate she could stand her ground. She never suffered fools gladly, which is something of a misnomer considering we were married for seventeen years. To Lesley, the fools of the world were those unable to see the beauty of life in what lay before them: the money-chasers, the high-flyers, the flash man and the fancy woman whose lives were consumed by an outer struggle rather than an inner peace. Such people never impressed her. She was not moved by their achievement, and especially if it came at the cost of what to her were the essential values of life: faith, hope and love, which were manifest in a strong family, good friends and a great church.

Lesley and I were great together. Made for each other, you might say. And today, if my life amounts to anything, it is due in a large part to the fact that the whole of my adult life has been spent in her company. She was my greatest friend and fiercest critic. Her level of discernment always left me amazed. What would take me a morning to make a judgement over, she could make in five minutes. She was truly amazing, and we were truly in love.

For the first ten years of marriage we had no children. The assumption on the part of many was that we couldn't have any. It wasn't true. We'd simply mastered the art of good contraception. We were having a great time. When

Charlotte did arrive, our lives were enriched beyond
measure. When she entered our world on the 3 January
2001 it was a blessed and happy day, one that is indelibly
etched on my memory. Lesley was destined to have a
child, yet would be cruelly robbed of the joy of seeing her
grow into adolescence and adulthood. She was a fantastic
mum and deserved better – much, much better. It was that
drive of motherhood that gave her extra courage during
the latter days of her illness. Several weeks ago, on one of
the regular visits by her GP, he asked why she fought with
such fortitude. He likened her attitude to that of Job in the
Bible. As weak as she was she responded with a question.
'Do you have any children?' she asked.

'No,' he replied, 'I don't.'

'Well, when you have, then you'll know,' was her
swift response.

Knowledge is better than gold, we read in the
Proverbs, yet for all our chasing for it we are forced, perhaps invited, to live with unanswered questions. Not that
Lesley had many; she chose not to ask, 'Why me?' She
lived with the pain, internalized much of it and processed
it through a deep resolve to draw from each day what was
offered and pour it out in selfless love to those around her.
Rather like the day we'd heard her tumour had started to
grow again. That evening, devastated by the news, we
received a call. A young teenager was in trouble; he'd run
away from home. We along with others were seeking rec-
onciliation between him and his parents. At 11 p.m. we sat
in church trying to help a family through their troubles. I
sat and listened to her speaking with them, seeking a way
forward. 'If only they knew,' I thought, 'what she'd been
through today.' They never would know, that's how she
wanted it to be; such incredible courage.

It's difficult to know where Lesley got her courage
from, since she never considered herself brave. Yet to my

mind she was braver then most. Certainly, these past four years have been hard. At times, impossibly difficult. Yet not without meaning, fulfilment and, dare I say it, yes, at times, laughter. When people spoke to her, often they'd refer to that bravery. 'I'm not brave,' she'd reply. 'Bravery is for those people who climb mountains, sail oceans or fight in wars.' Well, Lesley, that was your take on the matter. But for the record, I just want the world to know that in my eyes you were. God knows, you were so bloody brave and I'm proud of you.

As it became clearer that cancer might get the better of Lesley's health, it became more important that it didn't get the better of her attitude, or mine. I began to coin a phrase to help process our thoughts. It went like this: 'In life some things come to change you, other things to be changed by you; wisdom is in knowing the difference between the two.' As we got to the place where we couldn't change our circumstances, we made a conscious decision to allow them to change us, to refine us, perhaps even make us more Christlike. As a result, faith became more important than ever.

Entering the unknown is akin to walking into the darkness. To hear some preachers, you'd think the darkness was the preserve of the doubter or sceptic. As if some magical field might cover those of faith from the ills of the world. We never aligned ourselves to such nonsense – and still don't. We needed a faith where God was not removed from the darkness, but where he walked with us in it. Any suggestion that God might be unhinged from the process of suffering is not only an offence to the message of the cross, but also a deeply disturbing and grossly incompetent gospel that is more suited to the realm of myth and fairy tale than real-world faith.

It's after the prose of the philosopher has fallen silent that you need the rhyme of the poet to soothe the ills of the world. If God was not to eradicate the darkness, then we must conclude he can be present in it. We must engage with those who sought to redeem their suffering in order to make sense of their pain. And so we drew comfort from the Psalms, especially Psalm 139:

Where can I go from your Spirit?
Where can I flee from your presence?
If I go up to the heavens, you are there;
if I make my bed in the depths, you are there.
if I rise on the wings of the dawn,
if I settle on the far side of the sea,
even there your hand will guide me,
your right hand will hold me fast.

If I say, 'Surely the darkness will hide me
and the light become night around me,'
even the darkness will not be dark to you;
the night will shine like the day,
for darkness is as light to you.[33]

The inseparable reality of God's life in the midst of the darkness is what Lesley experienced. She fought and believed for it and found it. She was an inspiration. The words that Charlotte read became real in Lesley's life. Her faith was tested and tried, but for those who knew her, it was also tangible. God was her refuge and strength and became a present help in trouble.

It's on those long hard days, when words so easily fall to the ground and dissolve like snowflakes from the sky, you need something firm on which to stand, a hand to hold. Again, the poet takes precedence, skilfully pouring oil onto open wounds. For many years 'Gate of the Year' by Minnie Louise Haskins was displayed in our bedroom. Only now does the power of what she wrote touch deeply the soul.

I said to the man who stood at the gate of the
    year
'Give me a light that I may tread safely into the
    unknown.'
And he replied,
'Go into the darkness and put your hand into the
    hand of God
That shall be to you better than light and safer than a
    known way!'
So I went forth and finding the Hand of God
Trod gladly into the night
He led me towards the hills
And the breaking of day in the lone east.
So heart be still!
What need our human life to know
If God hath comprehension?
In all the dizzy strife of things
Both high and low,
God hideth his intention.

'The Gate of the Year' by Minnie Louise Haskins. ©
Minnie Louise Haskins, 1908. Reproduced by
permission of Sheil Land Associates Ltd.

Wednesday 23 July 2008
Tonight I stood at the bedroom window watching the
trees blowing gently in the wind as the sun fell peacefully on the day. Birds flew, and the sky turned a rich
golden colour on this warm summer's evening. Apart
from the occasional shouting from children in the distance, it was quiet. Behind me lay Lesley, sleeping in bed,
drugged too much to sense her pain, and weakened by
the activities of the day. Earlier she'd been fitted with a
syringe driver – another threshold crossed in the process
of dying in our western culture. All previous medication

is now stopped. Paracetamol: gone. Gabepentin: gone.
Keppra liquid: gone. Antibiotics: gone. All replaced by a
cocktail of new drugs professionally mixed and delivered at 2 mm. per hour. There will be no going back to
the old ways, no more fighting to get medicine in on
time, no more struggling with that white plastic spoon
which had become such a familiar item in the journey of
care. The former things have passed away.

As I looked out over our garden to the trees and
buildings beyond, my mind was taken back to a very
different summer in 2004 when this journey began. I
recalled standing in a different garden, that of Lesley's
parents, and chatting with her father about our latest
visit to the consultant in Sheffield. The storm clouds
were only beginning to gather back then and, though
anxiety lay low inside me, there was room for optimism. We were still a long way off a cancer diagnosis;
our trips to hospital were investigative and filled with
cautious hope. Today, it all seems like a very long time
ago.

Now, as night begins to fall on another day, I wonder
how many more days will be left for Lesley. I pray for a
peaceful end, but it's not guaranteed. She's had two further bleeds in the past twenty-four hours with the real
prospect of more to come, one of which could be fatal.
Otherwise she might have a massive stroke to bring her
time to an end, or she could simply fall into a deep sleep
from which she never recovers. Her face is pale, her
sleep disturbed by the occasional groan as she wriggles
for comfort on her soft air mattress. The room is peaceful, save for the occasional whirr from the syringe driver as it delivers its dose, and I offer my prayers to the
Father for his will to be done.

None of us holds jurisdiction over another person's
life. Lesley's time is now in God's hands.

Illness forces you to come to terms with your mortality in a way that nothing else does. Today, we stand to some extent removed from Lesley's pain. We enter as observers of another's suffering, we walk away relieved at our own health and life as imperfect as it may be. Yet more fool us, if we consider Lesley's journey to be in isolation to our own. What today reminds us of is that death is not simply individual, but also inevitable. We will all one day walk the pathway she has trodden and, as certain as night follows day, the sun will one day set on our lives too.

So thank you Lesley. Thank you for the love, the laughter, the joy and the pain. Thank you for the privilege of being your husband. Thank you for giving birth to our beautiful daughter who is such a remarkable reflection of your beauty. Thank you for your grace and faith which you carried with such ease and tranquillity. Thank you that I can stand today and speak about us. To be able to say there are no regrets save for the fact you were taken too soon.

Lesley did not want to die and she fought with every ounce of strength to live. She was brave, courageous and strong. She did not look for death, but she was prepared for it. In the words of the apostle Paul, she fought the fight, she finished the race, and she kept the faith. When you go to war there is no guarantee you will come back alive, but dying makes you no less a victor. Christian hope presents a faith that not simply takes us to the grave, but beyond it; that faith was hers. This is my firm conviction. This is Lesley's legacy to us all.

Tuesday 5 August 2008

With the funeral over and the events of the past week behind us, today was the first day of a different life. Earlier I'd popped into town with Val and Charlotte and, whilst they were looking at girlie things, went and tried on a pair of trainers. I turned round to get Lesley's opinion, but of course she was not there. I put them back on the shelf. After twenty-one years of being together, and seventeen of them married, I'd ventured out of the door knowing she would now only live on in memories and pictures, and my visit to Next underlined the reality. The thought was not only profoundly sad but also deeply terrifying. How on earth would I be, without her, as I began my new journey of learning how to live again?

Epilogue

You never anticipate being widowed at the age of 42. When Lesley and I walked down the aisle as relative youngsters back in October 1990 and made our vows before God and the congregation, we anticipated decades ahead of us; the thought of growing old together sat in our minds like an old rocking chair in a cosy room, looking inviting but waiting it's time for another day, whilst before us lay our life together. So when widowhood came like a strong gale on a dark winter's night it was a strange and disturbing position to be found in: too young to consider life over, unlike an elderly man after say fifty or sixty years of marriage, and yet too old to erase the past two decades and live as though they'd not been. A difficult position, and not only for me but for everyone who entered my world.

It was not only difficult, it was also unusual. And it's the fact that it's unusual which prompted consideration for publishing my diary. How do you deal with unusual situations? How do they affect your faith and shape your life? Can any sense be made of such terrible suffering and injustice? They are all valid questions.

I considered the best way to address these issues was in the context of the diary itself. Yet it was clear that further input was required and, after thought and discussion with friends, I decided to add an epilogue; this would enable me to leave the diary as I wrote it at the time, save for clarification to assist narrative flow. But other things did need to be written, like our need for a theology of suffering, the importance of living without regret, understanding the role of prayer, and loving through illness, without which this book could be in danger of two extremes – either an excessive fascination with the process of morbidity, or a hankering after sympathy. Neither approach works, nor warrants the trees felled to produce it.

The mystery of suffering

The one question standing out from all those asked over the course of Lesley's illness was, 'How are you, and how are you coping?' As a general rule it's asked by two categories of people: those who don't understand, and those who do. The only difference has to do with tone and timing. And the ones who get the truthful answer are those who have timed the tone of the question just right. Otherwise the response is always the same: 'Not bad, thanks. And how are you?'

On reflection I think it's true that suffering causes you to internalize your pain. You do literally go to ground and that is part of the coping mechanism. I also discovered that whilst it's internalized it is also processed, as if the pain is taken off to a lab somewhere to be worked through, the results of which will be published later. There is of course a real danger with suffering, and that is a loss of perspective; this is particularly true for people of faith. Suffering messes with faith in the same way that quantum physics messes with your brain; you feel there ought to be an answer there somewhere, but my God, it's taking a lot of finding! Furthermore, the way in which we have westernized faith has not helped.

I remember listening to a preacher talking about their life at a time when Lesley's prognosis was at a critical point. They spoke with eloquence and passion about God's goodness and went on to describe how they had been blessed in their marriage with children, homes, finances and health. In my mind I couldn't help but draw a comparison. If that is how God blesses, then what about us? Does that mean, since we were at the polar opposite, we'd been cursed? Are health, prosperity, happiness and possessions a sign of blessing, and poverty, unemployment, illness and singleness a curse? Does one demonstrate God's favour, and the other his disapproval? And were we living under the disapproval of God? It was a terrible dilemma and I began to wonder how many other people lived with this sense of burden. As if the suffering itself was not enough, must we also carry the signs of his disapproval through the illness? And yet I had always sought to live in a right way before God. Since the age of 16 I lived with a sense of call and vocation to the Christian ministry. I had tried to honour God through my life and actions. I knew I was far from perfect, but I was trying – honest I was. Yet for all that effort, for all those decisions, here we were facing the most terrible of times, and there I sat listening to someone who appeared to have had a charmed life. It didn't seem fair.

Later I contacted my old friend Steve Chalke. Part of the letter that follows highlights something of that dilemma as I sought to make sense of the situation we were in. I explained how the path of life had dramatically changed. 'Lesley's prognosis is terminal' I wrote, then went on:

We got MacMillan Services involved today. It's another step along a journey we have not chosen to take. It brings it all home; the reality, the destination – it all hangs, waiting its moment. No doubt it will come – and that from an old Pentecostal with a developed theology of physical healing. Truthfully, it was weighed in the balance and found wanting some time ago.

I'm not so sure about a theology of healing – a theology of suffering has a truer ring, it's just not as popular in the mainstream! For all our proclamation, I fear not even my charismatic brothers can take me to see too many miracles. When the stakes are high you need more than sentiment, empty promises and vain hope, regardless of how well intentioned they are; you require a more robust and, dare I say, biblical faith. I'm on a different journey now; it may not offer as many solutions, but it has taught me to treasure the questions and allows me to maintain my integrity. The likes of Yancey have become a devotional comfort over the past few years.

I recently read your article in *Christianity* about suffering. To some extent you will know that I have followed your life and ministry over the years and can see a deeper, more reflective and well-crafted writer emerge out of your honesty and humility. Your vulnerability sets you apart – maybe even gives you your edge. Certainly your choice not to hide from your pain and allow it to form your convictions carries with it the authenticity that people look for. It's scary to consider the thought that pain can be redemptive, but one can't help but feel that in the midst of it, somewhere mysteriously lies the presence of Christ. If he can't meet us in our darkest hour, then surely our hope is in vain.

The inspiration to write to him was in part due to the opening line of his article, 'The Pain of Gain', in

Christianity magazine, where he wrote: 'It has to be one of life's greatest ironies. The best literature, the best poetry, the best music, the best art, the best thinking, the best theology – they all seem to be born out of struggle and pain . . .'

For me, along with pain came a deep desire to make sense of suffering, to find some pathway that could redeem the chaos which the tumour had caused. Of course for most people the search for that answer is in physical healing. We were no exception; physical healing has to be the obvious first place to look for those answers. If Lesley could have been healed of her cancer then both the nature and tone of my diary would have been completely different, but she wasn't. In fact, one might be forced to question to what extent, if any, physical healing as a result of prayer or faith played in her life. Certainly I would have to ask that question in order to remain true to myself. I don't wish to become a sceptic, but the evidence against is pretty strong. That's not to say therefore there is no value in prayer; quite the opposite in fact. Prayer played a central role in both upholding and sustaining us during that long and difficult journey; it simply didn't manifest in divine healing which was a difficult truth to swallow, given my tradition as a Pentecostal. There were lots of 'proof texts' for us to turn to, offered from numerous sources; they simply didn't work in the way prescribed, like medicine dispatched from a divine pharmacy. One now questions whether the use of proof texts as a form of Christian practice is a somewhat overstated and dangerously flawed theology. The way we handle the ancient scrolls should be of primary concern to all who profess to teach the Scriptures, myself included.

But then, maybe we are looking in the wrong places to find answers. Until we have dealt with the subject of suffering we do an injustice both to the message of Jesus and the world into which it's delivered, one which is broken and scarred by suffering. Pain defines our world, and if we can't reconcile that truth with Christ's message then we are truly lost; we have nothing to offer to the terminal cancer patient, the orphaned refugee or the mother whose child has died of malnutrition. The fact that Jesus entered into our world in order redeem it is central to the faith we hold. As the French poet, Paul Claudell wrote, 'Jesus did not come to do away with suffering or remove it; he came to fill it with his presence.'[34]

Michael Mayne, as he diarized his own battle with cancer, said, 'Aristotle wrote that the main purpose of tragedy was to awaken pity and terror, together with a sense of awe at our potential, not simply to bear and not to be overcome by suffering, but to redeem it, to bring something good out of a dark time.'[35] His insight into the purpose of suffering is profound, since for the most part we are given to 'not to be overcome' by it, as if that was the best outcome. 'I won't let this disease get the better of me,' we hear people say, as if that were the point or purpose; but the mystery of suffering is about something deeper. Redemption is about much more than deliverance. It's about restoration. Suffering becomes redemptive when we see past the presenting issue and our pain becomes a means of connection to Christ rather than a dislocation from him. For what other reason could the apostle Paul have written, 'I want to know Christ and the power of his resurrection and the fellowship of sharing in his sufferings, becoming like him in his death' (Phil. 3:10).

Far from being removed from suffering, Jesus is fully engaged with it. He was a 'man of sorrows' and 'familiar with suffering' (Isa. 53:3). That familiarity helped shape his life and ministry in the same way that suffering should help to shape ours so we too become the conduits of grace – those who carry God's love and compassion into the brokenness around us. Yet even that is only part of the truth; suffering isn't important simply from the perspective of training, as if to say, 'Now I have suffered I have greater compassion for others.' It is important not as a means of equipping us to better help others, but as a means of redemption; suffering has the power to take us beyond ourselves, to stir the divine within, to remind us that we truly are made in the image and likeness of God.

Hugh Dickenson explains it well whilst writing to his friend Michael Mayne:

> I'm sure there is a humanity in God long before the appearance of *homo sapiens* – anything even faintly hominoid has a capacity for God to some degree. Us he can inhabit fully, and in so doing endures and groans and travails as part of the deal; including our despair. But something gets born in the darkness I know, something of which I become aware only much later, when to my own surprise I find I am changed. A sheer gift, that's unplanned, unexpected, and undeserved. I suppose that's what they mean by grace?[36]

Paul explains it in this way: '. . . since we have been justified through faith, we have peace with God through our Lord Jesus Christ, through whom we have gained access by faith into this grace in which we now stand. And we rejoice in the hope of the glory of God. Not only so, but we also rejoice in our sufferings, because we know that suffering produces perseverance; perseverance, character; and character, hope. And hope does not disappoint us, because God has poured out his love into our hearts by the Holy Spirit, whom he has given us'

(Rom. 5:1–4). It is the productivity of suffering which interests him. Paul sees something birthed through it that isn't found elsewhere, which leads to hope and lies at the heart of redemptive suffering.

Of course none of this makes sense outside of faith, because of the need for an eternal context. As C.S Lewis noted when referring to his own convictions, 'I believe in Christianity like I believe that the sun has risen, not simply because I see it, but because by it I see everything else.'[37] Hope is the substance of this eternal perspective – it allows us to see things that otherwise remain off-limits, and it's this alone which provides a context to begin to grapple with the mystery of suffering.

It was because of this idea about the mystery of suffering that for many years I struggled with the 'bless me' culture of the church which appears to have so much of its roots in a materialistic philosophy. The idea that God's favour is shown in health, possessions and prosperity always felt fundamentally flawed in my mind because of its inadequacy to recognize with any sense of reality the world in which we live. (Not that I have a problem with wealth itself; just the idea that it is the evidence of blessing.) How could this possibly be when the Bible sites such verses as "Has not God chosen those who are poor in the eyes of the world to be rich in faith and to inherit the kingdom he promised those who love him?' (Jas. 2:5) It is God's bias towards the poor and the oppressed which makes the gospel so glorious. He appears to err on the side of oppression as if he was more comfortable there and when Jesus comes, he is born not into the opulent setting of five-star luxury, but into the smelly surroundings of an animal's cave in Bethlehem.

It's a clue.

A clue to all that follows.

And not only that, but it also establishes the context for his Messianic ministry. Jurgen Moltmann wrote in his book, *Experiences of God*:

> This knowledge of the God who suffers with his people and wanders with his people's wanderings kept alive the hope of the Jewish people in suffering and the experience of death . . . This message, it seems to me, is also the message of the God who humiliated himself in Christ. 'Only the suffering God can help us', wrote Dietrich Bonhoeffer from his prison cell.[38]

Why? Because he has been where you are; the Christian message is not one of extraction but engagement, where divinity takes on humanity and walks amongst us. There is hope in our suffering, not because suffering is right, good or fair; there is hope in suffering because God can be found there. He is not sitting in an ivory palace removed from us, but on an executioner's cross suffering for us, and with us. This is the position from which we can engage with suffering, and the perspective from which we can begin to redeem it. Not some naïve triumph that denies the reality of our place in a broken world, but a position of camaraderie and comfort that allows us to walk through it upheld by God's grace.

The importance of living without regret

This is really important; please read what follows carefully because it matters.

It matters a lot.

There are far too many people who live and, sadly, die with regret. They are regrets about all sorts of things, like a love lost, or an opportunity not taken in career or business. People live with regrets about not having travelled enough, and then being too ill to travel, or regrets about putting off having children, or not spending enough time with the children they have. Regrets come in all shapes and sizes and some matter more than others. Like those I've listed, you read through them and think: well not all those regrets are the same. They don't all carry equal weight. It's true.

The art of a good life is to reduce controllable regret to an absolute minimum, which takes both time and effort. I say controllable regret because some regret you have to deal with falls outside of what you can control and needs a different response. The key to good regret control has to do with priorities and decision-making. If we make good decisions over the important areas of life then it reduces the amount of regret we live with, which in turn affects the level of stress we have and improves our quality of life.

When Lesley was very poorly I knew there would come a time when I would lose her. That sense of impending loss does all sorts of things to you, and affects you in every imaginable way. Dealing with those feelings is a large part of the journey. You start to think through every possible scenario including if there are any regrets in your relationship.

Thankfully, for me and, I believe, for Lesley, they were few, such as not taking her to Monaco. She had always wanted to go there, but for one reason or another we never quite made it. I also regret not having redecorated our bedroom, since she spent so many months in bed that it would have been nice if I had bothered to decorate all those years before when she asked me! But this is all manageable regret; it doesn't paralyze me going forward.

Conversely, now, as I look back, I also don't regret the amount of time I spent with her, the scores and scores of hospital appointments attended, the amount of time spent sitting in waiting rooms whilst she was scanned and scanned again; the countless hours spent on wards and then finally sitting with her, alongside her parents, in our own bedroom. I did moan about it inside at times, there were moments when I resented what the illness was doing to me as well as Lesley. How it interfered with my dreams, ambitions and 'career'. At other times it was hard to see other people getting on with life whilst we were just getting on with coping. Those things can be really hard to handle. But at the end of it all, I know I did my best, and it's because of that I live without regret. The smaller things don't really matter because the major items were in place.

Lesley's death has only served to heighten in my life the importance of not putting yourself in a position whereby regret becomes permanent and therefore potentially paralyzing through guilt. It reminds me of the well known song by Mike and the Mechanics, 'The Living Years'. Written by Mike Rutherford, it reflects the strained relationship between him and his late father and is a strong reminder, if one were needed, of the importance of dealing with issues rather than leaving them unresolved.

This next sentence is not easy to write. It's not easy to write for fear of misinterpretation, but since I have approached this book on the basis of complete honesty with myself and vulnerability with my readers, I will write it.

I have no regrets over Lesley's death and carry no guilt over life moving on, as I spoke at her funeral, 'There are no regrets, save for the fact you were taken too soon.'

I believe this is how regret should be handled in both life and death. It is an important lesson we do well to learn so that it doesn't dominate our present nor loom large over our future.

Loving through illness

Recently a friend told me about a colleague at work who contracted cancer and at the same time lost her husband to an affair with her best friend. Her prognosis was terminal and she died within six months, knowing that her children would be raised by the woman and husband who broke her heart. To her it must have felt like the ultimate betrayal, but she's not on her own.

In a Cancer Research supplement in *The Guardian*, people who had been affected by various forms of cancer were asked which were the most difficult aspects to deal with. The figures were: practical effects 13 per cent; physical effects 41 per cent; emotional effects 45 per cent. That's about right. To the question: have you experienced any difficulties in your relationship with your husband, wife or partner as a result of your cancer diagnosis, 26 per cent replied 'yes', a surprising 25 per cent had actually broken up, and a further 12 per cent had seriously considered it.[39]

Illness can be tough on relationships. I attended a wedding over the summer and listened to the young couple make their vows to each other 'for better, for worse; for richer, for poorer; in sickness and in health; till death us do part'. They each repeated them with utter sincerity, an occasional tear running down the cheek. Few of us really understand the depth of the vows we make, but at some point in the future they will be tested and that's when sincerity needs to adopt other virtues such as tenacity, commitment and self-discipline – love has more than one face.

A particular danger I found with Lesley's terminal diagnosis had to do with its destination. I remember speaking with a minister colleague who'd lost his own wife to cancer when his children were young. We spoke one day after a meeting we had attended. It would have been a couple of years before Lesley died, but at that stage we knew the seriousness of her condition. 'Illness is bittersweet,' I said, 'it brings out both the best and worst in you. It pulls you together, yet at the same time tears you apart.' He simply looked at me, lowered his tone of voice and agreed; it was the poet Keats who said that until something is experienced, it is not real.

One of the hardest things to handle is the two directions the disease takes you in. For one, it is a journey of dying, for the other, a contemplation of a life without your partner. They are lonely pathways which can separate the union of marriage. Up until that point, every decision is taken together, whether that is to do with a job opportunity, children, homes, finances or holidays. You sit together as a couple and have your discussions and make your plans. But with terminal illness it's different. It's not that you don't talk and share, not even that you don't enter into each other's fears and worries. For Lesley and me, we had many conversations about the future – about dying, about life after she had gone. But there are things that fall off-limits; areas that are too difficult or too sensitive to approach, and it's at that point you realize that illness can be a very lonely path to tread.

There is also a fear of being honest with other people about your own feelings. About what the illness is doing to you, as the healthy partner. About how they will view you if you confess to some of your darker thoughts. I was very fortunate in that respect, and had good friends who listened to me at various levels of confession and challenge. Without judgement, they would take moments to enter into my world and soothe my pain with their time and attention. No one can take it away from you, but being properly listened to does help. Their conversations didn't keep me faithful to my vows to Lesley – only I could do that – but they did keep me sane. I remember taking a walk round the local park with one such friend, and it taking almost to the end before I mustered the courage to tell him about one issue related to some thoughts I was having at the time. It was one of the most courageous things I have done, to bring a secret fantasy in my head that rolled round in the darkness, and drag it into the light. I was never unfaithful to Lesley, but that conversation reminded me of the dangers our journey could bring.

As an illness progresses, the way in which love is shown changes. The lack of physical intimacy which is a major rock in any marriage is obviously challenged, and that can be hard to handle; but it's not just about the sex. One day, whilst chatting with Jeremy, our former consultant, he said, 'Any cancer diagnosis is hard on a relationship, Stephen, but when it affects the head it is particularly difficult. Sadly, you start to lose the person you once knew. I'm so sorry.' I asked him how much longer he thought Lesley would live, he told me his thoughts, and I kept them to myself.

Yet even when the darkness closes in and the days get harder and longer, love is not lost. As Paul wrote, 'Love is patient, love is kind. It does not envy, it does not boast, it is not proud. It is not rude, it is not self-seeking, it is not easily angered, it keeps no record of wrongs. Love does not delight in evil but rejoices with the truth. It always protects, always trusts, always hopes, always perseveres. Love never fails' (1 Cor. 13:4–8a).

It always protects, always trusts, always hopes, and always perseveres.

The face of love for us was changing, but it was still love, and that couldn't fail.

In any relationship, love is measured by the way in which it meets the needs of those it treasures. As those needs change, the way in which love is delivered changes too. In the first flush of romance, love may be measured in fun and flirtation. It's about exploration and the deepening of a newly born relationship. Boundaries are established and challenged, adjustments are made and then adjusted again and, over time, those two people become one. But in illness or later life, love can take a different shape. The essence of what it is stays the same, still protecting, trusting, hoping and persevering, but the delivery system alters.

Over time I began to recognize how Lesley's needs were changing, and not only that, how she felt deeply saddened by the fact that she couldn't be all to me she had been in the past. Such times can become a breeding ground for pain and hurt, and so it is even more important to be careful with words and actions. Love doesn't always need to be demonstrative in order to be sincere, and is sometimes best measured and shown through time and tenderness. They are valuable lessons to learn. The gentle stroking of a forehead can be as meaningful as a passionate kiss, and the tender embrace after two decades of love can be as important as sex. Love is a virtue full of grace and beauty; its depth can immerse the deepest sorrow and cover over the harshest pain. Paul was right – love never fails.

The role of prayer

There was a time when God and I didn't speak for a while. Apparently he had nothing to say and frankly, neither did I. Now, he's big and I guess could handle it, but I'm small and couldn't, and it didn't seem fair that he should pitch his omnipotence against my mortality. During that period, prayer left me confused – hurting, even. I was confused by the apparent lack of intervention; that things just seemed to get worse for us. There was never any good news in which to find comfort.

I remember one day speaking to the congregation I lead: 'What disappoints me most about prayer is how God apparently has so much to say when I don't need to hear him, but then goes remarkably silent when I do. God appears to speak least when I need him most' were my rather crass remarks on an obviously grumpy morning. Now, in normal circumstances someone would have approached me afterwards and corrected my theology, but considering our situation, everyone remained silent. Either that or maybe they believed what I said to be true; that at times we all struggle with prayer and the silence of God is one of the frustrating mysteries of faith.

Philip Yancey in his book, *Prayer: Does It Make Any Difference?* opens with the quote, 'When a doctoral student at Princeton asked, "What is there left in the world for original dissertation research?" Albert Einstein replied, "Find out about prayer. Somebody must find out about prayer."'[40] The mystery of God's partnership with the human family is one of the main quests of faith. Can we truly and voluntarily trust God with our lives? Is he really there to meet us in prayer when we most need him?

Such questions go to the heart of what it means to believe, and have been the source of both inspiration and indignation for Christian people for centuries. That God would appear to intervene directly in some situations and not in others is enough to leave even the most dedicated follower confused, and if viewed this way reduces prayer to some form of spiritual lottery. So perhaps prayer is better viewed as God's interaction with, rather than intervention in, our lives. In this way prayer becomes the mystery of engagement where the human touches the divine, the place where, having got to our end, we discover we are at his beginning. As Alan E. Lewis wrote, 'To pray is to confess not the abundance but the exhaustion of one's verbal, intellectual, and spiritual resources, It is surrender'.[41] It is into this act of surrender that faith gently leads us. We enter into uncertain territory where doubt and fear lurk, with hope casting its light on a distant horizon. As we enter this new terrain, we go off in search of the hidden God, and if we look long enough we discover he is there to be found in the midst of pain and suffering, as scary as that sounds.

Yet of course none of this does anything to appease our desire for the immediate, or indeed the miraculous, which some people suggest ought to be the norm. Now, how you get to the place of the miraculous being the norm is, to my mind, something of an oxymoron. As C.S. Lewis said, 'That God can and does, on occasions, modify the behaviour of matter and produce what we call miracles is part of the Christian faith; but the very conception of a common, and therefore stable world demands that these occasions should be extremely rare.'[42]

And truth be told, we all know that that is exactly what they are – rare. But should the rarity of miracles therefore devalue the place of prayer? Only, I feel if we see our relationship with God as formulaic – if we ask in the right way, with the right faith, and hold on for long enough we will leave with the right results: healing, money, jobs, happiness and so on. I recently read some blurb for a book offering such solutions, promising to give real biblical reasons for sickness, and showing how it may be healed; that the Bible made it plain that all illness is given for a reason, and once that reason has been dealt with, the illness can then be taken away.

What? You mean all illness, gone, just like that?

Meanwhile, back in the real world, my own reading of the Epistles, which has to be the central source of teaching within the church, suggests that prayer has a more spiritual and transcendent role in our lives. It reminds us that we are tripartite beings with a hybrid nature. There is a correlation between the interrelated states of body, soul and spirit that makes up what it is to be human and, at the same time, living out what it means to carry the eternal flame within us. A flame that is fanned by God's Spirit and stirs our hearts with the noble theme of another life. As Paul wrote: 'But our citizenship is in heaven. And we eagerly await a Saviour from there, the Lord Jesus Christ' (Phil. 3:20).

Paul, like Jesus, appears to live from that other perspective. As such, the content of his prayers pays little respect to physical healing and outward manifestation, and more to inner transformation. The coming of God to us may at times include the miraculous, but more often will bring the transcendent. Consider this prayer, written to the church at Philippi: 'And this is my prayer: that your love may abound more and more in knowledge and depth of insight, so that you may be able to discern what is best and may be pure and blameless until the day of Christ' (Phil. 1:9,10). Or this really well-known prayer, written to the same church: 'Do not be anxious about anything, but in everything, by prayer and petition, with thanksgiving, present your requests to God.

And the peace of God, which transcends all understanding, will guard your hearts and your minds in Christ Jesus' (Phil. 3:6,7). The word 'transcends' reveals to us the role of prayer. It has the ability to take us beyond where we are. The translators have worked with the interpretation of this word into English, and it appears in various forms across the different versions of the Bible including 'passeth' and 'surpasses'. In essence, prayer is a transformational process at the heart of the individual, placing a guard over our spirit and soul. It is a means of growth, but not necessarily a guarantee of protection from the ills facing us in this fallen world. It connects us to God, but does not at the same time disconnect us from the effects of sin – that comes later in his redemptive story.

This idea of prayer connecting us to God is at the heart of the biblical message suggesting that he is journeying with us both through the good and bad times of our lives. Ever since Lesley first contracted cancer as a 15-year-old, she carried in her handbag a small version of Mary Stevenson's 'Footprints' poem that had been given to her at the time. The message captures something of what this journeying is all about.

In it the man has a dream where he sees his life depicted as footsteps in the sand. For part of the journey there are two sets of footprints but during the times of trial and difficulty he sees only one. He presumes that the dream is showing how he walked alone during those dark days, which concerns him and causes him to question God, only to discover that far from being alone, it was during those times that God was carrying him.

That sense of being supported through the trials of life is something which, I believe can be part of the journey of faith, and brings hope to even the darkest of situations. I remember speaking with a friend when Lesley was close to death; her journey had been long and arduous, and in my own life I had both retracted from, but now returned to, prayer as a source of comfort.

'Lesley might not be healed by our prayers,' I said, 'but she should certainly receive comfort through them.' From then on he joined me in praying that God would comfort her, that peace would come and that she would sense it. In truth, there were times when she sensed it more than others, but our focus from that time was clear. By now, I had moved some considerable distance from seeing comfort as second best to healing. The idea of God making us whole had a truer and more biblical foundation. It was finally something upon which life and faith could be built.

Recently, I was asked, 'Out of all the pain you have been through, what is there that you can offer to others? What can you give them that might bring comfort for people facing similar struggles to your own?' I thought long and hard about my answer. What could I say? I knew my faith was sustaining me. Why was that? It had made a difference, and more than that, so had prayer, and not only for me, but also for Lesley. There was a presence attached to our journey which I couldn't always identify that was not dependent upon my actions, or lack of them. It was about something deeper and more mysterious, it was about God's grace sustaining us.

Perhaps, like Paul writing to an anxious church in Corinth, we were experiencing the transcendent nature of our own and other people's prayers. He wrote: 'Praise be to the God and Father of our Lord Jesus Christ, the Father of compassion and the God of all comfort, who comforts us in all our troubles, so that we can comfort those in any trouble with the comfort we ourselves have received from God . . . On him we have set our hope that he will continue to deliver us, as you help us by your prayers. Then many will give thanks on our behalf for the gracious favour granted us in answer to the prayers of many' (2 Cor. 1:3,4,10,11).

In my mind, prayer had evolved from something that was prescriptive to something that was relational. Prayer did not necessarily bring answers, but it did bring perspective – and perhaps the most important perspective of all.

In the novel *The Shack*, by William P. Young, Mackenzie Philips' daughter is murdered whilst they are away camping for the weekend. Shattered by the news, Mack struggles to come to terms with the loss of Missy, his daughter. And one day he receives an invitation to return to the shack where her body was found. On his arrival he meets three characters who take on the incarnation of the holy Trinity, and so starts a long and fascinating conversation, where Mack is challenged over the facts of trusting a God of love, who only wants what is best for him – a God who is redeeming the world.

In this redemptive story, prayer plays its part, leading us through each chapter of life, with its twists and turns prompting the choices as to how we will respond to God. 'I have come to see prayer as a privilege', writes Philip Yancey[43] – the privilege being that it helps untangle something of the complex web of life, whilst holding in tension those unresolved issues for which we still have no answers. We may not have full resolution over those matters, but we can allow the peace and comfort that prayer offers to soothe our anxieties and fears. When suffering and pain leads us down a road less well travelled, the assurance from the Scriptures is of one who has been there before us and now comes to accompany us on that journey. That I found the comfort to be real and the peace to be wholesome is testament I feel to the role of prayer. Not my ability to be a praying person, but God's desire to walk with me in the often unspoken language of tranquillity, when all around the storms of life raged.

Now as I look back on those years and relive them through memories, I don't see prayer as something that was done at certain times of the day or night, or in particular ways or styles. Prayer was much more fundamental – not so much a state of action but of being, of walking through life accompanied rather than alone, drawing comfort from God's promise that regardless of the terrain we have to navigate, his commitment is to travel with us. As it is written, 'Never will I leave you; never will I forsake you' (Heb. 13:5).

If you have been affected by issues raised in this book and would like to contact Stephen you can write to him at:

Stephen Hackney
Hope Church Nottingham
30 Varney Road
Clifton
Nottingham
NG11 8EX

E-mail: admin@hopechurchnottingham.org

You can follow Stephen's blog at http//stephenhackney.wordpress.com

Endnotes

[1] C.S. Lewis, *A Grief Observed* (London: Faber & Faber, 1961).

[2] MRI is the abbreviation for Magnetic Resonance Imaging, a radiology technique that uses magnetism, radio waves and a computer to produce images of body structures.

[3] Nasopharyngeal tumour is a cancer originating in the nasopharynx, the uppermost region of the pharynx or 'throat', where the nasal passages and auditory tubes join the remainder of the upper respiratory tract.

[4] ENT – Ear, Nose and Throat.

[5] Maxillofacial surgery treats conditions relating to the head below the base of the brain.

[6] This is an abbreviation for multiple sclerosis.

[7] CAT is the abbreviation for Computerized Axial Tomography scan, an X-ray procedure that combines many X-ray images with the aid of a computer to generate cross-sectional views and, if needed, three-dimensional images of the internal organs and structures of the body.

[8] Trigeminal nerve – a main nerve which provides sensation to the face.

[9] Sylvain had spent several years in the UK but, having returned home to France, tragically died in a car accident

leaving his family and friends and everyone at the church stunned and in a state of shock.

[10] 1 Corinthians 4:20.

[11] Psalm 84:5,6.

[12] David Hind and Tim Hughes are both Christian songwriters whose music Lesley particularly enjoyed.

[13] Charis Life Church is the name of the church where I am the pastor. Charis is the Greek word for grace.

[14] PET: Positron Emission Tomography: A highly specialized imaging technique that uses short-lived radioactive substances to produce three-dimensional coloured images of those substances functioning within the body.

[15] Chemotherapy drugs are often used together for maximum effect. First line chemotherapy for head and neck cancer is fluorouracil and cisplatin. Amazingly, as soon as the cisplastin was administered you could smell the tumour breaking down in her breath, leading to quite some excitement at the time.

[16] The Clifton Shop is the charity shop which we run from the church as a place of connection in the community and a source of funding for mission.

[17] Psalm 43:5.

[18] Love Clifton was an event organized by the church, which involved a week of activities in the locality that included a Kid's Club, tidying the gardens of older people, and concluded with a community Fun Day.

[19] Queen's Medical Centre, University Hospital, NHS Trust Nottingham.

[20] Riley, James Whitcomb. 'The Complete Works of James Whitcomb Riley.' Great Literature Online. 1997–2011 http://riley.classicauthors.net/completeworks/completeworks87.html (14 Feb, 2011)

[21] Michael Mayne, *The Enduring Melody* (London: Darton, Longman & Todd, 2006), p. 121.

[22] Mark 9:24.

[23] The Lakeland Outpouring was a prevalent theme in the Christian media during those final months of Lesley's life. Based in Florida, nightly revival meetings were being held, and frequent reports of miraculous healings were commonplace especially through mediums such as the popular *GOD* channel network.

[24] *Christianity* magazine – a national publication targeting in the main the evangelical/charismatic stream of the church.

[25] *Joy* magazine is the official publication for the Assemblies of God denomination in the UK.

[26] Michael Mayne, *The Enduring Melody*, p. 209

[27] Psalm 9:9.

[28] Psalm 10:1.

[29] Philippians 2:1.

[30] Phlebotomist – a nurse specializing exclusively in taking blood from patients.

[31] 1 Peter 1:3–11.

[32] Isaiah 53:3.

[33] Psalm 139:7–12.

[34] From *The Enduring Melody*, Michael Mayne.

[35] *The Enduring Melody*, Michael Mayne, p. 174.

[36] The Enduring Melody, Michael Mayne, p. 80.

[37] www.brainyquote.com/quotes/quotes/c/cslewis162523.html.

[38] Jurgen Moltmann, *Experiences of God* (Philadelphia: Fortress Press, 1981), p. 17.

[39] This reference is taken from Michael Mayne, *The Enduring Melody*, p. 231.

[40] Philip Yancey, *Prayer: Does It Make Any Difference?* (Grand Rapids, MI: Zondervan, 2006).

[41] Quoted in Peter Greig's book, *God on Mute: Engaging the Silence of Unanswered Prayer* (Eastbourne: Kingsway Publications, 2007), p. 85.

[42] Quoted in Peter Greig's book, *God on Mute*, p. 118.

[43] Philip Yancey, *Prayer: Does It Make Any Difference?*, p. 9.